Software Cost Estimation and Sizing Methods

Issues and Guidelines

Shari Lawrence Pfleeger, Felicia Wu, Rosalind Lewis

Prepared for the United States Air Force

Approved for public release; distribution unlimited

PROJECT AIR FORCE

The research described in this report was sponsored by the United States Air Force under Contract F49642-01-C-0003. Further information may be obtained from the Strategic Planning Division, Directorate of Plans, Hq USAF.

Library of Congress Cataloging-in-Publication Data

Pfleeger, Shari Lawrence.
  Software cost estimation and sizing methods: issues and guidelines / Shari Lawrence Pfleeger, Felicia Wu, Rosalind Lewis.
     p. cm.
  "MG-269."
  Includes bibliographical references.
  ISBN 0-8330-3713-7 (pbk. : alk. paper)
  1. Computer software—Development—Management. I. Wu, Felicia. II. Lewis, Rosalind. III. Title.

QA76.758.P4797 2005
005.1—dc22

                                                           2004030691

The RAND Corporation is a nonprofit research organization providing objective analysis and effective solutions that address the challenges facing the public and private sectors around the world. RAND's publications do not necessarily reflect the opinions of its research clients and sponsors.

RAND® is a registered trademark.

Published 2005 by the RAND Corporation
1776 Main Street, P.O. Box 2138, Santa Monica, CA 90407-2138
1200 South Hayes Street, Arlington, VA 22202-5050
201 North Craig Street, Suite 202, Pittsburgh, PA 15213-1516
RAND URL: http://www.rand.org/
To order RAND documents or to obtain additional information, contact
Distribution Services: Telephone: (310) 451-7002;
Fax: (310) 451-6915; Email: order@rand.org

Preface

Software has played an increasingly important role in systems acquisition, engineering, and development, particularly for large, complex systems. For such systems, accurate estimates of the software costs are a critical part of effective program management. The practice of predicting the cost of software has evolved, but it is far from perfect. Military and commercial programs alike are replete with examples of software cost estimates that differ significantly from the actual costs at completion.

Rather than seeking the perfect cost-estimation method, this report recommends an approach to improving the utility of the software cost estimates by exposing uncertainty (in understanding of the project as well as in costing accuracy) and reducing the risk that the estimate will be far different from the actual cost. The two primary factors addressed in this report are the decisions made during the estimation process (such as which methods and models are most appropriate for a given situation) and the nature of the data (such as software size) used in the estimation process. This report acknowledges the presence and effect of risk in any software estimate and offers pragmatic strategies for risk mitigation.

The techniques described here are based on literature reviews and analysis of software estimation and risk, in addition to general lessons and guidance adapted from selected programs described by cost analysts interviewed at the Air Force Cost Analysis Agency (AFCAA). This study was sponsored by the Assistant Secretary of the Air Force (Acquisition), in conjunction with AFCAA. The AFCAA supports the Air Force Secretariat by conducting independent cost analyses, special cost reviews, and cost-analysis research for Air Force component organizations.

This report is intended to assist experienced cost analysts in reducing the risk of inaccurate cost estimates. It should be of particular interest to those organizations or agencies that use software estimates in the planning, budgeting, developing, and/or purchasing of software-intensive systems. Additionally, this report should be of value to those involved in research and analysis of estimation models and techniques.

The research was sponsored by the Principal Deputy, Office of the Assistant Secretary of the Air Force (Acquisition) Lt Gen John D.W. Corley. The project technical monitor was Jay Jordan, the Technical Director of the Air Force Cost Analysis Agency.

This report should be of interest to government cost analysts, the military aircraft and missile acquisition communities, and those concerned with current and future acquisition policies.

Other RAND Project AIR FORCE reports that address military aircraft cost-estimating issues include the following:

- In *An Overview of Acquisition Reform Cost Savings Estimates*, MR-1329-AF, Mark Lorell and John C. Graser used relevant literature and interviews to determine whether estimates of the efficacy of acquisition-reform measures are robust enough to be of predictive value.
- In *Military Airframe Acquisition Costs: The Effects of Lean Manufacturing*, MR-1325-AF, Cynthia Cook and John C. Graser examine the package of new tools and techniques known as "lean production" to determine whether it would enable aircraft manufacturers to produce new weapon systems at costs below those predicted by historical cost-estimating models.
- In *Military Airframe Costs: The Effects of Advanced Materials and Manufacturing Processes*, MR-1370-AF, Obaid Younossi, Michael Kennedy, and John C. Graser examine cost-estimating methodologies and focus on military airframe materials and manufacturing processes. This report provides cost analysts with

factors useful in adjusting and creating estimates based on parametric cost-estimating methods.

- In *Military Jet Engine Acquisition: Technology Basics and Cost-Estimating Methodology*, MR-1596-AF, Obaid Younossi, Mark V. Arena, Richard M. Moore, Mark Lorell, Joanna Mason, and John C. Graser present a new methodology for estimating military jet engine costs and discuss the technical parameters that derive the engine development schedule, development cost, and production costs, and present quantitative analysis of historical data on engine-development schedules and costs.

- In *Test and Evaluation Trends and Costs for Aircraft and Guided Weapons*, MG-109-AF, Bernard Fox, Michael Boito, John C. Graser, and Obaid Younossi examine the effects of changes in the test and evaluation (T&E) process used to evaluate military aircraft and air-launched guided weapons during their development programs.

RAND Project AIR FORCE

RAND Project AIR FORCE (PAF), a division of the RAND Corporation, is the U.S. Air Force's federally funded research and development center for studies and analyses. PAF provides the Air Force with independent analyses of policy alternatives affecting the development, employment, combat readiness, and support of current and future aerospace forces. Research is performed in four programs: Aerospace Force Development; Manpower, Personnel, and Training; Resource Management; and Strategy and Doctrine. The research reported here was conducted within the RAND Project AIR FORCE Resource Management Program.

Additional information about PAF is available on our web site at http://www.rand.org/paf.

Contents

Figures

Tables

Executive Summary

Introduction (see pp. 1–7)

Estimating the size and cost of software is a risky business. When software is a crucial component in numerous space, weapon, aircraft, and information technology projects critical to operations, as it often is for the Air Force, accurate estimates of software costs are essential. Because software size is usually the most influential factor in determining software costs, good estimates of size are critical to good cost estimation. Rather than seeking the perfect method for estimating size and cost exactly, a more realistic approach to improving estimation is to reduce the risks (that is, to anticipate likely problems) associated with improper sizing and costing of software.

Consequently, the goal of this report is to aid experienced cost analysts in understanding the sources of uncertainty and risk in sizing and costing software, and to provide insight into mitigating the risks when making choices about different sizing and costing options. We pay particular attention to the early stages of a project, when many of the factors needed to support estimation (such as the particulars of each system requirement) may be unknown or uncertain.

The notion of risk is central to any such analysis, and two techniques can improve accountability of risks relating to software estimates: identifying areas of uncertainty (that may lead to risky situations) and analyzing the estimation process to determine where risk mitigation can reduce the uncertainty. The first technique increases an analyst's diligence in reporting uncertainty. The second technique involves actually addressing and mitigating risks in the estimation process, thereby reducing the total uncertainty and increasing the estimate's accuracy. The two techniques are complementary. The first improves accountability by reporting the uncertainty. The second improves accountability by dealing with and reducing the uncertainty.

This document addresses both techniques, offering guidelines to cost analysts on how best to manage the unavoidable risks that are attendant on predicting software size and cost. These techniques inject realism into the estimation process, acknowledging that estimates are often made with limited knowledge of the system and a profusion of choices that may be rife with uncertainty.

Sizing Methods (see pp. 9–13)

Software size estimation is critical to providing a credible software cost estimate; thus, choosing the appropriate method by which to estimate size is important. In most cases, the estimation risk (that is, the possibility that the estimate will be far different from the actual software cost) depends more on accurate size estimates than on any other cost-related parameter. Thus, it is important that software sizing be done as consistently and accurately as possible, given the uncertainties inherent in estimation.

However, software sizing is difficult for a number of reasons. First, it is performed in a variety of different contexts,[1] some with a great deal of knowledge about the system and some with almost no knowledge at all. Second, there are many choices for the language and structure used to express the requirements and design. Third, software projects are often a combination of new, reused, and modified

---

[1] The context depends on the resources available to the project, the degree to which the developers are familiar with the problem to be solved by the software, the developers' expertise in the problem domain and with the development tools, and more.

components. A sizing method must be able to incorporate all three modes, even when the reuse and modification occur in the requirements and design instead of just in the code.

Both sizing and costing methods typically belong to one of two types, or a combination of the two types: expert judgment or measurable items. The expert judgment method relies on the ability of one or more analysts to determine the likely product size by evaluating the nature of the requirements, often in some qualitative fashion. Usually, the analysts have knowledge of similar development efforts, and the degree of similarity is relative to their understanding of the proposed project. By contrast, sizing based on quantitative, measurable items can use aspects of the requirements, such as number of requirements, number of transactions and screens, or other constructs (such as function points), to suggest the resulting size. With this approach, the size-estimation process is often more formal; the analysts are guided by questions or steps to elicit parameters from which the likely size is then calculated.

Advantages and Disadvantages of Sizing Methods

Several global issues should be considered when using a sizing method. We discuss them in the following categories (see pp. 13–22):

- Counting physical objects, such as lines of code or number of requirements. Advantages include ease of counting (and ease of counting automation), independence of programming language, ease of storage in a historical database, and ease of management understanding. Disadvantages include difficulty of counting early in the development process, dependence on programming or specification style, need for rigor in applying counting rules, and inconsistency of methods across different languages.
- Counting notional constructs, such as function points or application points. These objects may be easier than physical objects to define early in the development process, but as notional ideas they are often more difficult to track over the course of devel-

opment. Advantages include ease of generation from a clear specification and persistence across intermediate products (such as design or early code modules). Disadvantages include inconsistency as analysts interpret the notional constructs (leading to the need for careful and consistent analyst training) and the difficulty of assessing the size of embedded systems.

- Lack of empirical evidence, especially for new sizing methods. A new sizing method may be more appropriate for a new development technique than are existing methods, but there may not yet be empirical evidence available to suggest appropriate values for input variables.

- Using past project experience and information. Many estimation techniques rely to some degree on the availability of information about past projects. This reliance can leverage lessons learned on earlier projects and reduce variability in input values. However, seeming similarities may mask significant differences in the new project. In addition, historical information may not be in a format useful for a new sizing method.

- Tracking changes and progress over time. Using size to track progress may help to manage the expectations of developers and customers alike. But many sizing models are designed to be used at the beginning of development, not in the middle; a size estimate built from the factors related to one goal may be inappropriate when the goal changes. Moreover, different size measures generated over the course of development may not be comparable over time.

- Calibrating the model. Calibration tailors the model to an organization or development style. When the calibration is performed carefully, the resulting tailored models tend to be more accurate than all-purpose ones. However, new or radically different projects may not be estimated accurately from the calibrated model.

After discussing the ramifications of each issue, we describe seven different sizing methods that the analyst may use (see pp. 23–41). For each method, we present its sources or origins in software literature, useful references to related web sites and articles, and a description of how each method works, when to use it, and when not to use it. Included are the following:

- Source lines of code (SLOC): a method that estimates the total number of lines of code in the finished software project
- Function points and feature points: methods that measure the amount of functionality in a system by counting and weighting inputs, outputs, queries, and logical and interface files
- Object points: a method that measures size by high-effort items, such as server data tables, client data tables, and screens and reports reused from previous projects
- Application points: a method building on object points, adding rating scales of a project's productivity
- Predictive object points: a method also building on object points, adding information about how objects are grouped into classes
- Analogies: a method using other, completed projects with similar characteristics to the proposed project to suggest the likely size
- Unified Modeling Language (UML) constructs: a relatively new method based on use case, a technique for describing how users will interact with the system to perform functions.

For example, Boehm et al. (2000) revised the object-point approach for use in the COCOMO II estimation process. Calling their technique "application points" to avoid confusion with object points and object-oriented development, they added rating scales to determine a project's productivity in new object points per person-month, the development environment's maturity and capability, and the developer's experience and capability in using the development (integrated, computer-assisted software engineering, or ICASE) environment. That is, application points are an enhancement of object points, designed to include more information about the project and, thus, to reduce uncertainty. A table assists analysts in choosing a rating (from very low to very high) for each of the three additional scales; the ratings are combined with other ratings. Then the resulting application points measure acts as a size input to an effort estimate. The estimated number of person-months is calculated as the number of application points divided by the productivity measure in the table. Application points are to be used specifically with COCOMO II effort- and schedule-estimation models. There is no evidence that application points are useful in models other than COCOMO II. However, as other estimating techniques embrace the changes in COCOMO II, new evidence may support a decision to switch to application points for sizing.

Of course, all sizing methods have their advantages and disadvantages, depending on the level of knowledge about the system; variation in the languages and structures used to implement the system; and system composition (the use of new, reused, and modified code within a system). Selecting the appropriate size-estimation method helps mitigate the risks associated with each choice.

Risks in Size Estimation

Risk occurs at many points in a project's life cycle and is tied to activities or to timing. When a decision or choice is made (whether on the micro-level, such as how to design a particular software module or on the macro-level, such as which software architecture to employ), an element of uncertainty is introduced in the estimation process; this choice increases the risk and, thus, the chance for error. This uncertainty is further aggravated when cost estimates must be made very early in the project's life cycle. (See pp. 43–53.)

Thus, it is important to recognize the risks and deal with them properly. One source of estimation error is the presence of incorrect or incomplete data elements, such as descriptions of how the software will be developed or notions of how the user will use the software system. Another source of error derives from correct data being used incorrectly, as when a computation is not complete or is applied inappropriately. But these errors themselves are derived from three kinds of uncertainty: (1) in the specification or design, (2) about the development method, and (3) in the estimation process.

We consider the following risks important to each of the above categories:

- Uncertainty in the specification or design
  - Problems in understanding the requirements or design
  - Incomplete or inconsistent requirements or design
- Uncertainty about the development method
  - Economies and diseconomies of scale
  - Mismatch between the proposed development method and the estimation's assumed method
- Uncertainty in the estimation process
  - Subjectivity and lack of independence in the adjustment factors
  - Counter-intuitive values for adjustment factors
  - Adjustment factors that seem irrelevant to the current project
  - Rater bias
  - Inter-rater disagreements
  - Inappropriate use of measurement.

Each of these risks is described in terms of symptoms and warning signs; these, in turn, can alert the analyst to the possibility of risk, and we recommend mitigation strategies for each. For example, consider the risk of diseconomies of scale. Sometimes, techniques that have good effects in the small can have bad effects in the large. For instance, using formal methods to prove the correctness of requirements has been shown to find problems in requirements, but using formal methods on a large scale can be expensive, time-consuming, and sometimes infeasible. Symptoms of diseconomies of scale include inability to judge the effects of the candidate technology on the size of development and inability to decide which parts of the system should be subjected to the technology (such as deciding which portions of the requirements should be proven correct using formal methods). To mitigate this risk, it may be useful to decompose the system into subsystems and then do a size estimate for each subsystem. Such decomposition can be based on the work breakdown structure (WBS, a formal description of the tasks and their dependencies) or on functional subsystems, each of which will be developed in a different way.

In addition to describing each risk, we provide a risk checklist for size estimation to which an analyst may refer repeatedly throughout the project's life cycle. This checklist refers to three important stages in the project life cycle: selection of the sizing method, assessment of the project/system, and application of the cost-estimation method. In each of these stages, we suggest actions that may help the analyst to avoid risks in the short term and long term. (See pp. 55–59.)

Approaches to Cost Estimation (see pp. 61–76)

Sizing is only one aspect of estimating how much effort will be involved in developing, delivering, and maintaining software. We analyze the broader issues of cost estimation, acknowledging that cost estimation is as much an art as a science.

Cost estimates for software development and maintenance activities are frequently associated with decisions about affordability, investment, and value. *Affordability* includes not only the costs necessary to accomplish the development but also those costs that address training, repair, and upgrades over the intended system's life cycle. *Investment* decisions consider whether the associated costs will yield a specific capability within the time and resources available. *Value* may consider whether other options can provide a more affordable or less risky investment to achieve the desired capability.

Thus, the way in which a cost estimate is used often depends on the types of decisions that need to be made, when they are needed, and who is making them. In particular, we can view a cost estimate from the perspective of the system's buyer, developer, or user, as well as from the perspective of a researcher who is trying to analyze how well a model or technique meets intended needs. The different uses of cost estimates suggest that the inherent risks differ, based on perspective and need. Thus, the relationship of risk to cost estimation can be understood only with a concomitant understanding of how the estimation is performed.

To that end, we review several widely recognized methods for estimating software cost, from informal methods that rely heavily on experience and expertise, to very formal parametric methods based on formulas derived from past performance. The methods include expert judgment, analogy, parametric and algorithmic methods, bottom-up (work breakdown structure) methods, and top-down methods. For each method, we describe how it works, the advantages and disadvantages, and appropriate usage.

For example, methods using analogy rely on data from actual projects, thereby avoiding expert judgment's reliance on recall. They also avoid the complexity of parametric/algorithmic models. Templates can be built to characterize different kinds of projects or project attributes, to explicitly account for differences between previous projects and the proposed project. Tools, such as Bournemouth University's ANGEL (Shepperd and Schofield, 1997), can be used to support the estimation.

However, there are several disadvantages to using analogies. Because this method depends on expert judgment to account for differences and to extrapolate from a previous project to the current project, it can be challenging and subjective. Two projects that may seem similar may indeed be different in a critical way (just as a runner who runs a four-minute mile cannot run a marathon in under two hours). Moreover, the uncertainty in assessing similarity and difference means that two different analysts may have significantly different views and eventual estimates. This difficulty can be mitigated by using historical data, which in turn requires maintaining and using a database of templates or project data.

As with expert judgment, analogy is not suitable when the estimation analysts have neither experience nor data for similar projects. Similarly, the method is not useful when some aspect of the proposed system is dramatically different in some way from most of the other projects in the database or in the analysts' experience. However, analogies may be useful when estimates are needed from sparse, high-level system descriptions, particularly before detailed design or requirements are fully specified.

Each of the estimation approaches described can be enhanced by the existence and use of a historical database of project information. Not only can models be derived from such data, but the data are also essential for calibrating models, suggesting confidence levels, supporting expert judgments and analogies, and assisting any reality check of an estimate supplied to another source.

However, historical databases are like good hygiene: Everyone acknowledges that they are good to have, but not everyone follows through with careful practice. It takes time and effort to define the appropriate data elements, build a repository, gather and verify data, provide an effective interface to enable analysts to retrieve appropriate data, and use those data to build and calibrate models. In addition, the data may be proprietary or difficult to obtain by those maintaining the database. The costs related to the care and feeding of historical databases must be compared with the cost of generating poor estimates. In almost every case, the investment in historical data is well worth it (Boehm et al., 2000).

Risks in Cost Estimation (see pp. 77–89)

Much as with sizing error, error is introduced into the data and estimation process as a function of three types of uncertainty: in the system definition, in the system development, and in the estimation method. For each type, we analyze the indicators of risk and suggest steps to be taken to address it. For example, during system definition, the problem to be solved may not be well defined. Symptoms may include different interpretations of what is needed, substantial use of "TBD" or "TBS" (to be determined or supplied) in the specification, or constant change to the specification. If the system use is not well understood, the concept of operations may be incomplete, inconsistent, or ambiguous. And, if the system is pushing the limits of technology, key requirements or functions may be included in the program risk plan. To address these risks, the likely cost can be expressed as a range, not as a point estimate; several estimates can be made over time, and estimation assumptions can be challenged repeatedly.

Similarly, risk is introduced during system development. Uncertainty in the development process is indicated when critical-path activities are unknown or unresolvable, or when there is lack of evidence that the developers are heeding or will adhere to software management plans. Other indicators of uncertainty are lack of consideration of the trade-off between maintaining a component or rebuilding it from scratch; lack of anticipation of potential defects; a mismatch between key personnel's experience and current needs; and lack of information about the consequences of possible loss. These system development risks can be addressed in several ways, including conducting several estimates over time, requiring having details on developing-organization performance, using historical data to support decisionmaking, and reviewing program documentation.

Estimation-process risk is introduced during method selection, application, and interpretation, and it can be addressed at several stages of the estimation process. When methods and tools are selected, warning signs of risk include lack of consideration of system characteristics (such as development approach, complexity, or size), intermediate results inconsistent with analysts' experience or expectations, or a mismatch between model goals and analysts' needs. During data collection, warning signs include insufficient information for use with the estimation model or inconsistent data inputs. When analysts review and evaluate a model's results, an unreasonable picture of likely cost and schedule is a signal that the model has been used improperly or is inappropriate for the situation.

Several steps can be taken to address these risks effectively. They range from garnering as much information as possible about the project to taking time to understand what methods each model uses, and whether those methods/models are appropriate to the project at hand. In addition, the developers can ensure that staff is trained on how to use each model. Cost analysts must be able to understand and document all the assumptions of their selected estimation model.

Well-trained cost analysts can generate reasonable estimates for each model variable, preferably in advance of examining the contractor data. If possible, they can conduct a sensitivity analysis on those key variables that engender significant uncertainty. Where possible, analysts can use multiple models to "triangulate" a reasonable estimate. In addition, they can verify reasonableness with expert judgment.

Other risk-reduction measures include using correct and appropriate economic data, such as cost rates for personnel, to support each model input. Analysts should pay careful attention to the scale or units required for each variable, such as constant dollars or dollars adjusted for inflation. In addition, they should understand whether and how each method or model considers maintenance costs and time, and adjust accordingly. Wherever possible, analysts can simplify models by concentrating on using inputs with the most effect and eliminating inputs that have very little effect on the resulting estimate. The effect of each input can be assessed retrospectively by performing a sensitivity analysis on each input; those inputs whose differences yield little change in the overall estimate can be eliminated in future estimates.

By developing and retaining a repository of historical data and metrics, cost analysts can use the data to support realistic inputs, to check the realism of outputs, and to provide feedback, learning, and comparison.

Final Directions (see pp. 91–92)

The information provided in this report can be used in two ways: to address techniques for improving current estimation methods and to find new methods when existing ones prove inadequate. The latter function is particularly important. Software development is changing, reflecting not only the need to find better ways to build better software but also the market pressures to use different technologies as they are proposed by the research and commercial communities.

An inaccurate estimate does not always mean a bad estimating technique or an incapable analyst. Instead, it may mean that the technique must be calibrated or extended, or that the analyst may need refresher training. In the end, the combination of method selection and analyst's action helps to mitigate avoidable risks in estimating software size and cost.

CHAPTER ONE

Introduction

The Air Force Cost Analysis Agency (AFCAA) supports the Air Force Secretariat by conducting independent component cost analyses, special cost reviews, and cost-analysis research. To these ends, AFCAA is organized as four separate estimating divisions and one cost-research division:

- Aircraft and Weapons Division, with the mission of developing estimates to support proposed aircraft, guided weapons, and missile systems.
- Information Technology Division, with the mission of developing estimates for information technology projects.
- Space Technology Division, with the mission of developing estimates for space-based Air Force projects.
- Force Analysis Division, with the mission of developing factors and performing estimates focused on long-range planning. This division also develops and maintains the Air Force Total Ownership Cost (AFTOC) database, a repository of historical information about estimates and costs that is useful in informing future cost estimates and cost-related decisions.
- Research and Resource Management Division, which provides support to these technical divisions.

The analysts in the technical divisions use a host of estimation tables and tools to generate cost and schedule estimates for hardware and software. All divisions have a common interest in improving software-estimating tools and in producing more-accurate software cost estimates.

Every cost estimate is inherently risky, in that an analyst must predict likely cost when there is much unknown about the software to be built. That is, since a risk is a problem that may occur during development, the analyst is asked to anticipate problems with development before development has begun. At the stage at which the estimate is being made, it may not even be known which staff will build and test the software, or what kind of design will solve the problem described by the software requirements. Thus, the notion of risk is central to any cost analysis. In particular, since the size of a software system is uncertain until development is completed, the risk of estimating size incorrectly is a major component of the risk of inaccurate cost estimates.

This document focuses on the role of risk in producing size estimates (used as inputs to software cost and schedule estimates) and the cost estimates themselves. Intended for use by experienced cost analysts, the document addresses how to manage the risks inherent in selecting and using a particular estimation method, especially at the early stages of a project, when many of the factors needed to support estimation may be unknown or uncertain.

Rather than seeking a universal, one-size-fits-all size- or cost-estimation method, this report supports a careful analysis of factors that affect the accuracy of the estimate. In particular, the two key factors addressed in this report are the decisions made during the estimation process (such as which methods and models are most appropriate for a given situation) and the nature of the data (such as software size) used in the estimation process.

Two techniques can improve accountability of risks relating to software estimates: identifying areas of uncertainty (that may lead to risky situations) and analyzing the estimation process to determine where risk mitigation can reduce the uncertainty as the estimate is produced. The first technique increases an analyst's diligence in reporting uncertainty by recognizing that uncertainty is inherent in any estimation but oftentimes goes unreported. For example, managers sometimes expect to be given a point estimate—the software will cost x dollars—when, in fact, the best that can be said is that the cost will lie within a given feasible range, characterized by a particular distribution. The distribution itself expresses the degree of uncertainty in the estimate: A narrow distribution is less uncertain than a wide one, and the distribution's shape imparts additional information about the likely cost. The capture, quantification, and reporting of that uncertainty give greater credibility to the estimation.[2]

The second technique is to actually address and mitigate risks in the estimation process, thereby reducing the total uncertainty and increasing the estimate's precision. This technique examines the estimation process itself to identify each choice at each decision point in what makes up a decision tree. Then, each point is analyzed to determine what risks are inherent in making each choice. Every possible path through the decision tree represents a set of risks, and management can associate with each path a set of actions to mitigate the risks whenever possible.

The two techniques are complementary. The first technique improves accountability by reporting the uncertainty. The second technique improves accountability by dealing with and reducing the uncertainty. This document addresses both techniques, offering guidelines to cost analysts on how best to manage the unavoidable risks that are attendant on predicting software size and cost. These techniques inject realism into the estimation process, acknowledging that estimates are often made with limited knowledge of the system and from a profusion of choices that may be rife with uncertainty.

---

[2] Uncertainty is inherent in the choice of distribution. Sometimes, data seem to follow a standard distribution, such as a logarithmic or Poisson distribution. At other times, a distribution is generated from historical data. However, uncertainty diminishes only when there is a solid explanation for why the data follow a particular curve. For example, Norden and Bakshi (1960) showed that the time histories of research and development projects suggest that effort follows a Rayleigh curve. Putnam (1978), reading Norden and Bakshi, noted that software-development effort seems to follow a similar curve; however, only anecdotal evidence supports this observation.

Study Methodology

This study's primary objectives were twofold: to provide a general assessment of the risks involved in software cost estimation and to provide strategies to mitigate those risks. In support of these objectives, the research contained four tasks, each of which was accomplished by literature review and analysis. Where applicable, the reviews incorporated lessons from sample programs to develop pragmatic risk-mitigation strategies. The four tasks were (1) understanding the concept of risk as it applies to software cost estimation, (2) examining why and how risk occurs in software estimates, (3) detailing the options for choosing estimation techniques and their required inputs when developing estimates, and (4) developing strategies and options to mitigate risks. We describe each task in turn.

1. Risk and Software Cost Estimation

We began by establishing a taxonomy for terms such as *uncertainty*, *error*, *risk*, and *accuracy*. Risk is usually expressed in the form of confidence levels and confidence limits. *Confidence level* refers to a statistical percentage of certainty; for example, "At the 95-percent confidence level, we can say that our cost falls between X and Y." This statement expresses the fact that, statistically, there is a 95-percent chance that the true cost of the system falls between the given confidence limits X and Y. This expression of risk is an indication of how accurate the estimate is believed to be. However, the factors that drive this accuracy (or lack thereof) are uncertainty and error. Thus, understanding the sources of error and uncertainty was addressed in the second task.

2. Sources of Risk in Software Estimates

We explored the relationships among risk, error, and uncertainty by asking the question, "Where are the sources of error in software cost and schedule estimates?" By decomposing software estimation into three basic components—select method, collect data, and apply method—we developed a basic model for error. Error can be introduced with the data (that is, with the estimation model's inputs) or with the estimation process (that is, by way of the decisions that are influenced by the system definition, system development, and the estimation method). We used existing literature and program experiences to characterize these errors and the underlying uncertainties. Two areas—sizing software and using cost models—warranted detailed descriptions to facilitate the application of risk-mitigation strategies. They were addressed in Task 3.

3. Options in Developing Estimates

We described each of the major approaches to sizing and cost estimation, so that the analyst could compare and contrast the methods when making a decision about which method is most appropriate (or comparing the results from two different methods). Our descriptions are based largely on our review of existing literature.

4. Strategies for Risk Mitigation

We concluded this study by developing checklists to codify the recommended practices, guidance, and lessons learned for reducing the uncertainty and errors in the areas of risk that we identified. Because the checklists address the similarities among software projects but not their differences, they are neither complete nor comprehensive. Rather, they provide a useful framework and an initial set of strategies upon which to build. They must be augmented periodically by new research and actual program experience. Other augmentations might involve additional quantitative information to help an analyst determine which risks are more likely or are of greater consequence.

Report Organization

To describe and analyze the risks, this document is organized in several chapters. Chapter Two begins with a discussion of two important issues related to estimation: the meaning of estimation quality, and the differences among the concepts of error, risk, and uncertainty. Following that discussion is a description of some of the major issues analysts must consider when selecting and using a sizing method.

Then Chapter Three focuses on current sizing methods, including what each is, how to use it, and what its output is likely to be. The document contrasts the different methods, laying out their pros and cons in terms of such issues as how much uncertainty is inherent in using the method, and whether the method relies on historical data or previous experience. In Chapter Four, the issues, the pros and cons of each method, and the information about risks and uncertainties are then organized as a risk checklist, so that an analyst can see what risks are inherent in choosing a particular sizing method and in using it in a particular way. This checklist can be applied to an existing or proposed sizing method to help assess its appropriateness or usefulness in a given situation. Chapter Five presents the risks again, reorganized to help an analyst review an existing size estimate and determine whether the estimate has addressed all relevant issues.

The remainder of the document addresses the more global risks inherent in cost estimation. Cost analysts must produce software cost estimates for a variety of programs. Ideally, the estimated cost will prove to be very close to the actual cost, and several estimation models purport to be flexible enough to provide accurate estimates in almost any situation. Unfortunately, this ideal is far from the reality. In fact, some models work best when restricted to particular situations or when applied using databases tailored to an organization's particular experiences.

A more realistic approach to software cost estimation involves understanding the differences among models as well as the risks inherent in selecting one model over another. The findings highlighted in this report are intended to aid cost analysts in managing the risks inherent in providing software cost estimates, in two key ways:

1. By discussing the pros and cons of various cost-estimation methods
2. By providing a concise risk checklist that can be applied to an existing or proposed cost-estimation method to help assess its appropriateness in a given situation.

To these ends, Chapter Six describes the characteristics of different techniques used to provide estimates and the role of historical databases in supporting estimation. Focusing on the risks inherent in cost estimation, Chapter Seven details the sources of risks and errors, presenting risk-related checklists that cost analysts can use in performing an estimate and for evaluating the estimates of others. Finally, Chapter Eight summarizes the way that cost analysts can use the notion of risk to guide estimation decisions.

CHAPTER TWO

Balancing the Advantages and Disadvantages of Sizing Methods

Given that size is the principal determinant of cost in most cost-estimation models, an accurate size estimate is crucial to good cost estimation. We explore the several major approaches to sizing and the different sizing methods in Chapter Three, noting here that many of the methods share common advantages and disadvantages. In this chapter, we discuss several aspects of size estimation and the pros and cons to be considered when selecting a method. This discussion makes visible the issues involved when identifying the risks inherent in estimating size. Chapters Four and Five build on this basis, by highlighting risks and suggesting strategies to mitigate them.

Because accurate size estimates mitigate risk more than any other cost-related parameter, it is important that software sizing be done as consistently and accurately as possible, given the uncertainties inherent in estimation. Although analysts like to think that they can remove risk by improving accuracy, the more realistic hope is that analysts learn to manage risk by understanding, exploring, and (wherever possible) reducing the uncertainties involved in producing estimates.

Several issues make software sizing difficult. First, software sizing is performed in a variety of different contexts, some with a great deal of knowledge about the system and some with almost no knowledge at all. For a new project, the sizing estimate must be done at or near the very beginning of a project, before the actual software is written and, often, before the requirements are finalized. In this case, sizing usually involves some kind of translation from entities, characteristics, and relationships in the requirements or design to the likely size of the code once it is written. The nature and correctness of the translation are major factors that need to be addressed.

For projects that have already started, some of the software may already be written but require additions, changes, and deletions, as in a major satellite development program in which the system was already four years into development when AFCAA was asked to estimate the cost of completing the software. In such cases, and when operational software is being maintained, the sizing estimate must take into account not only how much software must be changed but also how knowledgeable the developers are. When the maintainer is not the person who built the original software, changes may take longer; the maintainer needs time to understand the existing requirements, design, and code before designing and implementing changes. Thus, the sizing estimate must include not only the direct changes but also any "scaffolding" software needed to evaluate, change, and test the existing software.

In the middle of a project, it is useful to examine the immediate prior history of that project to manage the expectations of the remainder. For example, when analysts on the above satellite system considered the projections for the size of the software at completion, the contractor-supplied estimates included a significant amount of reuse. In particular, at project start, a tremendous amount of reuse was predicted, based on the claim that "it was the same system; it was just being rehosted." However, the originally predicted levels of reuse were not achievable; the software size grew considerably as the system was implemented. This past experience was useful in determining future projections about the size of the remaining software; as a consequence, the predicted levels of remaining reuse were reduced.

Second, there are many choices for the language and structure used to express the requirements and design. For example, requirements can be written as English-language descriptions, as formal specifications (using mathematical expressions), or as use cases (part of the Unified Modeling Language). They can be organized in paragraphs, in linked charts, or in tables provided by software-requirements repositories such as RequisitePro. Any translation from these expressions to software size has to be consistent enough to yield correct size estimates, no matter how the requirements and design are captured. By *consistent*, we mean two things: When the translation is done by two different analysts or tools, their results are approximately equivalent; when the translation is done from two different expressions of the requirements or design, the results are essentially the same.

Third, software projects are often a combination of new, reused, and modified components. A sizing method must be able to incorporate all three modes, even when the reuse and modification occur at the requirements and design levels, instead of just at the code level. These categories are particularly important when sizing is done in the middle of development (especially when the software is being developed iteratively or incrementally) or to support the estimated cost or schedule for a proposed maintenance change.

Deciding which sizing method is most appropriate in a given situation also involves a number of factors, including

- Ensuring that the assumptions of the sizing model match the conditions under which the software will be built
- Using the model as it was intended
- Tailoring the model (often by calibration) to the special needs of the organization using it
- Understanding the probability distribution that describes the likely software size.

These aspects of sizing are commonly considered to belong to cost or schedule estimation. But, in fact, they are aspects of sizing, too, since some of the size-estimation methods require using a model that is manipulated using adjustment factors, analogies, or historical databases. For example, a sizing technique may recognize that one line of code is not necessarily the same as another: The effort expended in writing one line may be markedly different from that used to write another. Sometimes, for instance, code that implements an algorithm may be more complex and require more time to design and test than one that simply describes the characteristics of a data item. A sizing technique can be based on a model of which types of lines of code contribute the most to the effort needed to write the system. Or a technique may require tailoring to the type of system being developed, such as transactional or real-time.

Characterizing Sizing Methods

We can characterize sizing methods as belonging to one of two types: based on expert judgment or based on measurable items. The expert-judgment method relies on the ability of one or more analysts to determine the likely product size by evaluating the nature of the requirements, usually in some qualitative fashion. For example, the experts may notice that a proposed system is the same as systems they have built or estimated in the past. Sometimes this estimate is generated by drawing analogies between the proposed project and previously completed ones, using as the underlying assumption that, even when systems are different, similar characteristics in the requirements suggest similarly sized systems when development is complete.

By contrast, sizing based on quantitative, measurable items can use aspects of the requirements, such as number of requirements, number of transactions and screens, or other constructs (such as function points), to suggest the resulting size. With this approach, the size-estimation process is often more formal; the analysts are guided by questions or steps to elicit parameters from which the likely size is then calculated.

A historical database of sizing information can be used to enhance either sizing approach. As projects are specified, developed, and completed, managers can capture information about them in a repository that later is accessed by others. The database can store not only the sizing information but also project and system descriptions to support determination of which projects or subsystems are similar to completed ones. The database can also contain counts of related elements, such as function points, requirements, or Unified Modeling Language (UML) components.(See Chapter Three for a more detailed description of techniques that use these elements.) And it can store information about how the system changed over time, helping analysts to understand whether, when, and how a system is likely to change.[3]

When to Use a Sizing Method

Although most people think of generating a size estimate at the beginning of a project in order to help estimate the effort and schedule, managers and estimation analysts can, in fact, use size at several points during the development process: to scope a project and support bidding, to assist project managers in allocating resources once the project is approved, to track progress and evaluate productivity, and to analyze the impact of proposed changes. We examine each use in turn.

When a project is first proposed, a size-estimation method is used to scope the project during bidding. A size estimate provides a general sense of how large the considered system may be, suggesting how many resources (including people and time) are needed to build the system and thus providing essential input to the bid. To determine whether the bids are reasonable, cost analysts can evaluate the bidders' sizing methods for appropriateness and accuracy by examining the inputs and estimates (and comparing them with similar projects in the historical database, if such a database exists).

Next, a size estimate derived by estimation analysts during requirements elicitation can help managers in two ways:

- To manage expectations about each requirement, in terms of what adding a requirement will mean to the overall project size
- To weigh priorities among requirements, helping to avoid "gold plating" some requirements (that is, adding unnecessary or unnecessarily complex requirements) that can be achieved more simply and cheaply.

---

[3] One such effort is being conducted by the Defense Cost and Resource Center, sponsored by the Director, Program Analysis and Evaluation, under the Secretary of Defense (http://dcarc.pae.osd.mil).

Similarly, a size estimate provided during design can help managers assess whether the designed system is far more or less ambitious than was envisioned earlier in the project.

In the midst of development, estimation analysts can assist project managers by predicting the likely size of the finished product, thereby helping them to determine whether the project is on track—that is, whether the software will be completed and delivered on time. Since the requirements and design may change as more is understood about the problem being solved by the software, it is not unreasonable to reestimate size after requirements and design modifications have been approved. Similarly, the size estimate can help evaluate productivity, not only to determine whether the project team needs help but also to assist in decisions about reorganizing project resources.

Finally, size estimates generated during maintenance assist managers in deciding whether and when proposed changes should be made. Each change can be viewed as a modification to requirements and design. A size estimate for each alternative can support project managers as they weigh the pros and cons of making changes.

We can summarize the concerns about sizing methods by considering several key issues that affect the degree of risk in adopting a method and, therefore, the likely accuracy and utility of the method.

Issue: Counting Physical Objects

Some of the sizing techniques, such as source lines of code, rely on a straightforward count of physical objects, in the sense that the analyst can count actual characteristics rather than assess general notions. For example, some sizing models base the size of modified, reused code on the size of the existing programs as expressed in number of modules or number of lines of code. Other models use modules or lines of code from similar projects. The advantages of this type of technique are as follows:

- The measurements are easy to make and usually involve counting particular markers, such as end-of-line designators or number of use cases.

- Automation of this approach is easy, since the items counted are well defined and easy to extract from actual products.
- The counting methods are not necessarily dependent on the programming language that is eventually used to implement the system. Instead, they rely on types of characters or constructs, such as semi-colons, blank lines, or use cases. Thus, there is little risk that two different people or programs will generate dramatically different counts from the same system specification—as long as the same constructs are generated in describing the system.
- Measures such as number of semi-colons or blank lines are easily stored in a historical database.
- The measurements are easy for management to understand and track, because they are related to tangible or visible things.

However, disadvantages include

- Dramatically different specifications resulting from variations in programming or specification style can lead, in turn, to very different size estimates for the same system.
- Rigor needed in counting rules. Counting rules must be exact, clear, and complete. Any ambiguity leads to suspect size estimates.
- Inconsistency of methods. There may be different rules for different languages or constructs, so it is difficult to compare size estimates across methods. For example, it is particularly difficult to compare lines-of-code estimates with estimates based on UML. Similarly, when systems are developed in more than one language, the size estimates may not be comparable. And comments embedded in code written in one language may not be comparable to comments in another.
- Statement counts. Care must be taken to ensure that measuring the number of programming-language statements adequately captures the size as reflected in the language. For example, expression-based languages such as C and C++ may generate low statement counts, thus yielding a misleading size estimate.

Issue: Counting Notional Constructs

Because there are few physical or visible objects to examine early in the development process, it is often appealing to use notional constructs, such as the amount of "functionality" (expressed as function points or application points), to generate size estimates. Such techniques have advantages and drawbacks.

In their favor are the following:

- The constructs can be generated from a well-written and complete specification. Thus, the size estimate is available early in development.
- The notional construct can persist, even when the expression of the intermediate products changes. For example, the notion of functionality can be derived from the requirements, then from the design, and then from the code, even though the requirements, design, and code may be expressed in different languages or models.

The drawbacks to notional constructs are as follows:

- Even when cost analysts are trained in assessing functionality (as with function points, for instance), managers sometimes have a difficult time relating to measures that are not tangible. For example, they do not see the connection between function points and working code.
- Because the notions are not observable or tangible, it is essential to train the counters to recognize and distinguish the notional constructs. The uncertainty in understanding and evaluating the notions can lead to inconsistent counting and wide variation across counters or across similar products. For example, Low and Jeffery (1990) evaluated the way in which function-point counters generated estimates. They found that there was a 30-

percent disagreement among raters for the same software requirements.[4]

- It is difficult to use notional constructs to capture the size of complex or embedded systems.
- For those sizing methods that eventually translate notions to lines of code, the method of translation can be subjective and particularly difficult if multiple languages are involved in the implementation.

Issue: Lack of Empirical Evidence, Especially for New Sizing Methods
There is little empirical evidence that project effort correlates most strongly with one particular kind of size measure, such as physical lines of code. For this reason, it is often better to use multiple size estimates and then evaluate the differences.

For an existing sizing method,

- The actual size of past projects can be compared with current estimates to determine the general accuracy of the method.
- The model on which the method is based can be revised to reflect the realities of using the method.

On the other hand,

- The method may be based on a model of development that is not the same as the one for the proposed project.
- The method must be "tuned," or calibrated, to the project for which it is about to be used.

For a new sizing method, the model on which it is based may profess to be appropriate for the proposed project, and new variables (describing other aspects of system development) may be introduced if they are consistent with the model's view of development. However, there may be little empirical evidence to allow comparison

---

[4] The inconsistency in function-point counting continues to be observed. See, for example, MacDonell et al. (1997).

of estimates with actual values, because the new model is too new to have generated a history of its accuracy.

Issue: Using Past Project Experience and Information

Some of the sizing methods rely to some degree on the availability of sizing information from past projects. Even expert judgment (particularly in using analogies, but also when using other sizing models) relies on the assumption that the expert can supply parameters based on understanding of similar, past projects. This reliance can have several advantages:

- The new estimate can leverage lessons learned on earlier projects.
- A historical database of project characteristics and size helps to keep variability down.
- Experience with a wide variety of past projects helps to keep variability down.

However, there are several disadvantages to relying on past experience and information:

- The experience and information may not be useful for new and very different projects. Worse, when apparent similarities mask significant differences, the experience and information may be misleading. For example, extrapolating from a less-than-four-minute mile leads to expectations of running a marathon in less than two hours—something that has never been done because the two races are significantly different.
- Projects often use different measures, techniques, tools, and processes, so comparing information can be difficult. For example, some counting techniques include requirements analysis in the time line for development schedule, but others do not.
- Historical project information may have been provided at the beginning of a project, as the project was planned. But it may not have been updated to reflect what really transpired.

Issue: Tracking Changes and Progress over Time

Size estimates are often made repeatedly during a project's lifetime. Cost analysts can provide early size estimates to help managers decide whether and how to do a project, but later estimates have different goals. The subsequent estimates can assist managers in evaluating proposed changes (in requirements, in design, in how to do incremental or iterative development, or in adapting to changing resources levels) or in tracking progress to determine how much of the project is actually completed and when intermediate and final products can be delivered. At the same time, the project itself can change substantially; consequently, the initial size estimates are no longer valid because the project has been reorganized or its goals have changed. In this case, the size must be reestimated to support management decisions about changing resources and methods.

The tracking can be done using a project database that stores not only the inputs to the size model or models but also similar information from past projects. This historical information can be used to suggest input for future estimates and also to check the validity of new estimates, based on past experience.

There are advantages to using size estimates to track change and progress:

- A historical database of past project information can bolster confidence in the estimates, particularly if the justifications for revised size estimates are maintained.
- Using size to track progress keeps estimates realistic and helps to manage the expectations of all project participants, including customers.

However, using size estimates to track change and progress has several possible disadvantages:

- Sizing models are based on assumptions about how the development process works. Many of the sizing models are designed to be used at the beginning of the development process, not during development. When size estimates are needed in the middle of development, such as when requirements change or when a major design consideration has changed, the objective of the estimate changes. For example, the early estimates may support bid/no-bid decisions, whereas the later estimates may support resource-allocation and intermediate product-delivery decisions. Similarly, sometimes a development team plans to reuse design or code components from other products. An early size estimate anticipating significant reuse may be useful for bid/no-bid decisions, but it may not easily incorporate changes in the way reuse is done as developers discover the need to modify more code than was originally planned. Thus, a size estimate built from drivers related to one kind of goal may be inappropriate for an estimate with a different kind of goal.

- Different methods for measuring size may not be comparable. For example, the level of granularity may change from one size-estimation process to another. The first estimate, done early in development, may measure the number of components, whereas subsequent estimates may have finer granularity and focus on lines of code. Similarly, measures of functionality later in development may be finer-grained than early measures of functionality, simply because more is known about a system later in the life cycle.

- Each sizing technique is usually defined to be used at a particular part of the life cycle; it may be difficult to find the appropriate inputs at subsequent stages of a project, when those inputs are not as meaningful. For example, some techniques, such as COCOMO (Boehm's Comprehensive Cost Model), use different size-estimation methods at different stages of the life cycle; tracking progress from one stage to another is far more difficult than is tracking changes.

- The size estimates may not be useful for new and very different projects or when the nature of a single project changes substantially. When changes are tracked on a radically different kind of project, the significant changes may not be visible to those who have little experience with them. Similarly, when the nature of a project changes, the analysts may recognize the changes only well after the fact. For example, if analysts used to evaluating transaction-based systems are asked to estimate size for real-time sensor software, the analysts may not recognize the elements of the new system that are key contributors to size. Likewise, when changes are proposed, the analysts may not realize that apparently small changes to the requirements can call for very large changes to the software.

• To compare estimates over time, the tasks and deliverables must remain relatively stable. Otherwise, successive estimates are not comparable because they are not based on the same project description. This problem is particularly pertinent for systems that rebaseline during development.

Issue: Calibration

Every estimation model must be calibrated to reflect the particular characteristics of the project team that will use it, including the development process and organization. Such model tuning ensures that the size estimate is derived from appropriate data—that is, from characteristics of projects, products, or resources that are similar in some way to the size being estimated. Thus, the calibration method relies on the availability of consistent rules for tailoring the sizing model to available data.

The calibration is usually performed by the cost analysts. The cost analysts will either be using a model or method for the first time or they will be maintaining the model or method after many uses, during which the development process has evolved. In the first approach, the initial model or method is derived from data that reflect a general situation as perceived by the model's developer; alternatively, a model-generating technique is demonstrated by using particular data, and the technique must be reapplied to the cost analyst's situation. Many commercial models represent the first kind of approach; they often include steps for "tailoring" the model to the cost analyst's situation. In the second approach, the sizing method may change over time; for example, consider how the notions of reuse or use cases have evolved over the years. COCOMO represents the second approach; originally derived from TRW data in the 1970s, it must be carefully calibrated to use current data.

The calibration activity is difficult if there are few projects with which to calibrate or if one or more characteristics vary significantly from one project to another. Moreover, the resulting calibrated model may focus on the norm or typical situation, leading to situations in which extremes are difficult to predict. Thus, there are two sides to calibration.

The advantages include the following:

- Calibration results in a model tailored very specifically to an organization or development style. Such a model is usually more accurate than general, all-purpose models that are less sensitive to the idiosyncrasies of a particular organization.
- Calibrated models can often be modified to include input variables and considerations that more-general models cannot tolerate.

However, there are two drawbacks to using calibrated models:

- New or radically different projects may have no historical database or baseline project from which to draw.
- Calibration must be done carefully; an improperly calibrated size model can easily lead to an incorrect estimate.

A cost analyst must consider these general issues carefully when deciding which estimation technique to use and how best to apply it to the situation at hand. In the next chapter, we examine each of the particular approaches to estimating size. Then, with an understanding of the various approaches, we turn in Chapters Four and Five to a recasting of these issues in terms of risks, likely outcomes, and mitigation strategies.

CHAPTER THREE

Survey of Sizing Methods

In this chapter, we describe seven representative sizing methods: lines of code; function points and feature points; object points; applications points; predictive objective points; analogies; and estimating from UML constructs. Each description forms its own section and is brief. It is intended as an overview of what the sizing method is, not a complete tutorial on why it is valid or how it should be used. The description is meant only to allow the reader to understand the differences among methods so that the comparison of methods discussed later in Chapters Four and Five makes sense.

The description of each method is organized in five parts:

- **Source.** The seminal work that first described the size method or the comprehensive document that describes how the method works.
- **References.** Additional sources of information about the size method, including papers, books, and web sites.
- **How the method works.** An overview of the general principles supporting the method.
- **When to use the method.** The context for which the method is best suited, because each method is appropriate in a particular context.
- **When not to use the method.** Situations in which using the method would be inappropriate or misleading, because there are instances where the method should never be used.

Lines of Code

Source: Park, Robert E., *Software Size Measurement: A Framework for Counting Source Statements*, Pittsburgh, Pa.: Carnegie Mellon University, Software Engineering Institute, CMU/SEI-92-TR-20, September 1992.

References: Carleton, Anita D., Robert E. Park, Wolfhart Goethert, William Florac, Elizabeth Bailey, and Shari Lawrence Pfleeger, *Software Measurement for DoD Systems: Recommendations for Initial Core Measures*, Pittsburgh, Pa.: Carnegie Mellon University, Software Engineering Institute, CMU/SEI-92-TR-19, September 1992.

Fenton, Norman, and Shari Lawrence Pfleeger, *Software Metrics: A Rigorous and Practical Approach*, 2nd ed., Florence, Ky.: Brooks Cole, 1996.

How the method works: This method attempts to assess the likely number of lines of code in the finished software product. Clearly, an actual count can be made only when the product is complete; lines of code are often considered to be inappropriate for size estimates early in the project life cycle. However, since many of the size-estimation methods express size in terms of lines of code, we can consider lines of code as a separate method in that it expresses the size of a system in a particular way.

Figure 3.1 illustrates how characteristics of the system are transformed into a lines-of-code count. Although counting lines of code in the finished product seems straightforward, it can be quite difficult in fact. The difficulty stems from deciding what to include as a line of code. For example, developers often build "scaffolding" code: code used to test and evaluate the system but not delivered with the final product. This code may include stubs and drivers (code used temporarily during testing to represent not-yet-completed parts of the system), requirements or design prototypes, and debugging code to print out intermediate results. Since lines of code are used as an input to estimating the effort required to build a system, it can be argued that scaffolding code should be included in the size estimate because the

Figure 3.1
Transforming Characteristics into Lines of Code

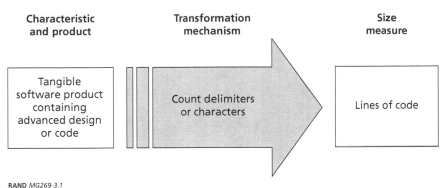

| Characteristic and product | Transformation mechanism | Size measure |

Tangible software product containing advanced design or code

Count delimiters or characters

Lines of code

RAND *MG269-3.1*

development team needs time and resources to build and use the scaffolding.

Comments (internal notes describing what the code is doing) present a similar problem. Although they are not executed, the comments are useful for explaining to developers and maintainers the reasoning behind the code's format and function. Code without comments is far more difficult to fix and upgrade, and comments certainly require time and effort to write. So it can be argued that a line of comments should be counted in a size estimate.

Reuse must be considered in the size estimate, too. Often, requirements, designs, code, and/or tests from previous projects or commercial applications are used as-is or modified, instead of constructing new ones from scratch. The purpose of this reuse is to save development time and resources. But reuse is not free; time is needed to find and assess the reusable components, as well as to modify those components to fit the needs of the new system. A lines-of-code estimate must take the nature and extent of reuse into account.

For these reasons, lines of code are often described as being source lines of code (SLOC) or source-delivered instructions (SDI). The former takes into account scaffolding code, whereas the latter reports only the number of executable lines of code in the delivered software product. Boehm's COCOMO models use SLOC as a size estimate, as do many others. Often, effort-estimation models will ask for non-commented SLOC. SDI are often counted automatically by the compiler; however, these lines of code can still be misleading. For example, macros (shorthand for small pieces of code) that are expanded only at run time may not have their lines of code counted.

Lines-of-code estimates are often made with the assistance of historical databases of size information. Early in the development cycle, it is very difficult to know what the actual number of lines will be. But similarity in requirements or design can be used as a link between the proposed system and well-understood completed systems. Thus, information from historical databases can reduce the uncertainty in early estimates of lines of code.

The Park reference, above, contains detailed templates that are useful for considering all the issues related to counting lines of code.

When to use the method: As inputs to effort and schedule models, size estimates are usually carefully prescribed. It is essential to use the lines-of-code counting method exactly as the effort and schedule models expect them to be used; otherwise, the size input will invalidate the effort and schedule estimates. Clearly, the later in the development process the lines-of-code estimate is made, the more likely it is that the estimate will be accurate (since more information is known about the actual product).

When not to use the method: A great deal of uncertainty is inherent in a lines-of-code estimate, simply because this type of estimate is an informed guess of the size of a product whose characteristics are not yet understood. Thus, it is important to use lines of code as a size estimate only when there is supporting information to reduce the uncertainty. That is, the lines-of-code estimate should not be used if it is a wild guess with no basis in past analogous products or performance. Neither should it be used if its basis does not conform to the counting rules prescribed by the cost- or schedule-estimation model into which it is input.

Function Points and Feature Points

Source: Albrecht, Allan J., "Measuring Application Development," *Proceedings of the IBM Applications Development Joint SHARE/ GUIDE Symposium*, Monterey, Calif., 1979, pp. 83–92.

References: An automated function-point calculator is available at http://www.engin.umd.umich.edu/CIS/course.des/cis525/js/f00/ artan/functionpoints.htm.

International Function Point User's Group information about certifying counters, using the method, and more is available at http://www.ifpug.org.

International Function Point Users Group, *Function Point Counting Practices Manual*, Release 4.1.1, Princeton Junction, N.J.: International Function Point User's Group, 2001.

International Function Point Users Group, *Guidelines to Software Measurement*, Release 1.1, Princeton Junction, N.J.: International Function Point User's Group, 2001.

A mapping from function points to lines of code is discussed in Allan J. Albrecht and John E. Gaffney, "Software Function, Source Lines of Code, and Development Effort Prediction," *IEEE Transactions on Software Engineering*, Vol. SE-9, No. 6, November 1983, pp. 639–647.

Information on feature points is provided at the web site for Software Productivity Research: http://www.spr.com.

How the method works: Function points were developed by Albrecht (1979) at IBM as a way to measure the amount of functionality in a system. They are derived from the requirements. Unlike lines of code, which capture the size of an actual product, function points do not relate to something physical but, rather, to something logical that can be assessed quantitatively.

As shown in Figure 3.2, the function-point metric is calculated in two steps. First, a table like Table 3.1, which captures both data and transaction information, is used to calculate an initial function-point count. For each row, the count in column 2 is multiplied by the appropriate weighting in columns 3, 4, and 5 to yield a number

Figure 3.2
Transforming Requirements into Function or Feature Points

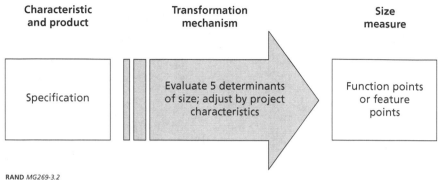

RAND *MG269-3.2*

Table 3.1
Initial Function-Point Count

Type of Input	Count		
	Simple	Average	Complex
Number of external inputs	3	4	6
Number of external outputs	4	5	7
Number of external queries	3	4	6
Number of internal logical files	7	10	15
Number of external interface files	5	7	10

that is supposed to represent the amount of functionality contributed by that row. The five weighted numbers are then summed to yield an "unadjusted function point" count.

The second step is to adjust the initial count by using characteristics that make the project more or less difficult than a typical project. The project is characterized by using a six-stage scale—no influence (weight of 0), incidental (weight of 1), moderate (weight of 2), average (weight of 3), significant (weight of 4), or essential (weight of 5)—to answer each of the following 14 questions:

1. Does the system require reliable backup and recovery?
2. Are data communications required?
3. Are there distributed processing functions?

4. Is performance critical?
5. Will the system run in an existing, heavily used operational environment?
6. Does the system require on-line data entry?
7. Does the on-line data entry require the input transaction to be built over multiple screens or operations?
8. Are the master files updated on-line?
9. Are the inputs, outputs, files, or inquiries complex?
10. Is the internal processing complex?
11. Is the code designed to be reusable?
12. Are conversion and installation included in the design?
13. Is the system designed for multiple installations in different organizations?
14. Is the application designed to facilitate change and ease of use by the user?

The weights are then applied to the unadjusted function-point count to yield an adjusted function-point count.

Albrecht and Gaffney (1983) translate function points to lines of code for use in cost- and schedule-estimation models. The translation differs, depending on the language to be used for development. The International Function Point User Group trains function-point counters and, as new languages are introduced, updates the translation tables.

Function points were enhanced in 1986 by Capers Jones at Software Productivity Research (http://www.spr.com) and named feature points. SPR's feature points add an algorithm parameter to the five existing function-point parameters. The algorithm parameter is intended to capture the functionality offered by an algorithm, as opposed to data or transactions; it is assigned a default weight of 3. The feature-point method also changes the weight for logical files (average) from 10 to 7 (Software Productivity Research, n.d.). Feature points are intended to expand the sizing method's applicability beyond data-processing systems to more complex, real-time systems.

When to use the method: Function and feature points address the need to generate a size estimate from those data available early in a project's life cycle. They can be valuable for providing a size estimate to an effort- or schedule-estimation method. Although the scientific basis for function points is suspect (because it is not clear which constructs contribute the most to effort; neither has the basis for the adjustment factors been shown to be complete and sufficient), the technique provides a common language and format for talking about size, especially when multiple languages or layouts are expected in the final product.

Function points were initially created for data-processing applications, so the five elements that contribute to unadjusted function points are best suited for those kinds of systems. Feature points may have wider applicability.

When not to use the method: Function- and feature-point counters undergo extensive training to enable them to count properly and consistently. Thus, inexperienced counters should not use function and feature points. As noted above, function points were developed for data-processing applications. They are not particularly well suited for real-time or embedded systems, since the elements that capture size for data processing are not the same as those for more complex systems. The literature suggests that, when systems are complex or embedded, those estimation techniques that are tailored to the particular constructs of the application domain (such as transactions in a transaction-processing system or sensors in a sensor data-fusion system) are the most-promising bases for estimating size.

Although function and feature points can be valuable for providing a size estimate to an effort- or schedule-estimation method, they are not useful for determining the project's status. That is, it is not valid to say that a certain percentage of the system is done if that percentage of function points has been coded, because additional effort is needed to integrate the functions together.

Object Points

Sources: Banker, R. D., R. J. Kauffman, and R. Kumar, "An Empirical Test of Object-Based Output Measurement Metrics in a Computer Aided Software Engineering Environment," *Journal of Management Information Systems*, Winter 1991–1992, Vol. 8, No. 3, pp. 127–150.

Kauffman, R. J., and R. Kumar, *Modeling Estimation Expertise in Object-based CASE Environments*, New York: New York University, Stern School of Business Report, January 1993.

References: Stensrud, Eric, "Estimating with Enhanced Object Points vs. Function Points," *Proceedings of the 13th COCOMO/SCM Forum*, Los Angeles, Calif.: University of Southern California, October 1998.

How the method works: As shown in Figure 3.3, this technique applies to all kinds of software development. Despite its name, it is not tied to object-oriented development. Using the same philosophy as function points, the object-point approach hopes to capture size in terms of items that require a high degree of effort to construct, such as number of server data tables, number of client data tables, and the percentage of screens and reports reused from previous projects. Object points synthesize a procedure suggested by Kauffman

Figure 3.3
Transforming Characteristics into Object Points

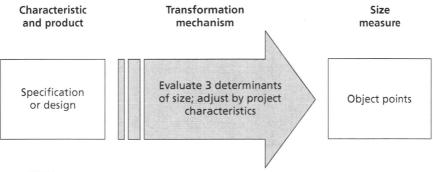

and Kumar (1993) and productivity data reported by Banker, Kauffman, and Kumar (1991). The latter paper reported that object points correlated with effort much better than did function points. The first paper noted that the average time to produce an object-point estimate was 47 percent of the corresponding time to produce a function-point estimate.

To compute object points, the analyst begins by counting the number of screens, reports, and third-generation language (3GL) components (that is, reusable pieces of software) that are likely to be in the application. In this way, object-point calculation is similar to function-point counting. Next, each object is classified as "simple," "medium," or "difficult," as shown in Table 3.2. The bottom part of the table contains the weight used in doing the final calculation.

As with function points, the weighted elements are summed. Although there is no set of adjustment factors, reuse is taken into consideration. If the analysts decide that r percent of the components will be reused from previous applications, then the number of new object points is reduced accordingly:

$$\text{Reuse-adjusted object points} = \frac{(\text{Estimated object points}) (100 - r)}{100}$$

$$(3.1)$$

When to use the method: Object points are useful only when the requirements or design are detailed enough to permit reasonable estimation of the input elements, such as when the number of screens, reports, and 3GL components is known. If the information is available, preliminary research (Stensrud, 1998) suggests that object points are preferable to function points. However, the technique is relatively new; there is no long-term history of the success or appropriateness of object points.

When not to use the method: As with many other sizing methods, object points are inappropriate if the analyst is working with inadequate information that could lead to wild guesses instead of informed estimates. Moreover, the input elements are similar to

Table 3.2
Object-Point Calculation

	Number and Sources of Data Tables		
	Total < 4 (<2 servers, <2 clients)	Total 4 to 8 (2–3 servers, 3–5 clients)	Total 8+ (>3 servers, >5 clients)
For screens: Number of views contained in tables			
< 3	Simple	Simple	Medium
3 to 7	Simple	Medium	Difficult
8+	Medium	Difficult	Difficult
For reports: Number of sections contained in tables			
0 or 1	Simple	Simple	Medium
2 or 3	Simple	Medium	Difficult
4+	Medium	Difficult	Difficult
Object Type	Simple	Medium	Complex
Screen	1	2	3
Report	2	5	8
3GL Component	—	—	10

function and feature points in that they are oriented more for data-processing applications than for real time systems or systems with tight performance requirements.

Application Points

Source: Boehm, Barry W., Chris Abts, A. Winsor Brown, Sunita Chulani, Bradford K. Clark, Ellis Horowitz, Ray Madachy, Donald Reifer, and Bert Steece, *Software Cost Estimation with COCOMO II*, Upper Saddle River, N.J.: Prentice Hall, 2000.

References: Pfleeger, Shari Lawrence, and Joanne Atlee, *Software Engineering: Theory and Practice*, 3rd ed., Upper Saddle River, N.J.: Prentice Hall, 2005.

How the method works: Application points are an enhancement of object points, designed to include more information about the project and, thus, to reduce uncertainty. Boehm et al. (2000) revised the object-point approach for use in the COCOMO II estimation process. Calling it "application points" to avoid confusion with object points and object-oriented development, they added rating scales to determine a project's productivity in new object points per person-month, the development environment's maturity and capability, and the developer's experience and capability in using the development (integrated, computer-assisted software engineering, or ICASE) environment. Table 3.3 presents an example of how this additional information is used in the model.

The application points act as a size input to an effort estimate. The estimated number of person-months is calculated as the number of application points divided by the productivity measure in the table.

When to use the method: Application points are designed to be used specifically with COCOMO II effort- and schedule-estimation models.

When not to use the method: There is no evidence that application points are useful in models other than COCOMO II. However, COCOMO II is relatively new; as other models derived from COCOMO (such as REVIC) embrace the changes in COCOMO II, new evidence may support a decision to switch to application points for sizing.

Predictive Object Points

Source: Minkiewicz, Arlene F., *Measuring Object-Oriented Software with Predictive Object Points*, report for Price-S Systems, available at http://www.pricesystems.com/downloads/pdf/pops.pdf.

Table 3.3
Application Points

Developer's experience and capability	Very low	Low	Nominal	High	Very High
ICASE maturity and capability	Very low	Low	Nominal	High	Very High
Productivity measure	4	7	13	25	50

References: Chidamber, Shyam R., and Chris F. Kemerer, "A Metrics Suite for Object-Oriented Design," *IEEE Transactions on Software Engineering*, Vol. 20, No. 6, June 1994, pp. 476–493.

Booch, Grady, *Object-Oriented Analysis with Applications*, 2nd ed., Redwood City, Calif.: Benjamin Cummings, 1994.

How the method works: This method takes advantage of the characteristics of object-oriented development. Using measurements suggested by Chidamber and Kemerer (1994), the technique is based on a measure called "weighted methods per class." In object-oriented development, the software is usually organized into objects (things) and methods (actions done by or to those things). Objects that have the same or similar properties are grouped into classes. The classes themselves are organized as a hierarchy, in which some classes can be parents of child classes that inherit characteristics from the parents. The number of methods per class measures the number of actions that can be taken by or imposed on the objects in the class.

The weights used in "weighted methods per class" relate to the notion of complexity. Chidamber and Kemerer leave the definition of complexity open so that the developers can choose a complexity measure appropriate for the project. For example, complexity may be measured by using the number of variables that the method uses or the number of transformations that the method makes. Then, weighted methods per class is calculated as:

$$\text{weighted methods per class} = \sum_{i=1}^{n} c_i \qquad (3.2)$$

where c_i is the complexity measure for method i (where there are n methods in the class). That is, we sum the set of method complexities to find the total weighted methods for the class. If the complexity of each method is 1, then the weighted methods per class is simply the number of methods in the class. The number of methods and the complexity of methods suggest the amount of time and effort needed to build and maintain the class. The larger the number of methods, the more effort and the greater the impact on the children of the class.

Predictive object points use the weighted methods per class as the basis for the size measure. Weighted methods per class are adjusted using information about how objects and methods are grouped into classes, as well as the relationships among classes and objects. The information is viewed along three dimensions—functionality, complexity, and reuse—and incorporates these measures:

- Number of top-level classes: Based on the hierarchy of classes, this measure counts the number of classes at the highest level of the hierarchy.
- Average depth of inheritance tree: The hierarchy can be viewed as a tree, in which there is a branch from a parent class to each child class. The tree can be traversed from the top to all of the children that inherit characteristics from it; the tree is called an *inheritance tree*, and the length of this traversal is called the *depth of inheritance*.
- Average number of children per base class: This measure captures the number of children (the leaves) in each of the classes at the top level of the tree.

When to use the method: This size measure is appropriate only for object-oriented development and only when enough is known about the application to be able to specify it in object-oriented terms.

When not to use the method: The predictive object point count is not appropriate for non-object-oriented development, and it is not useful very early in the project life cycle. It may not be useful in comparing projects when the measures of complexity (used for weighted methods per class) differ from one project to another.

Analogies

Source: Shepperd, Martin, and Chris Schofield, "Estimating Software Project Effort Using Analogies," *IEEE Transactions on Software Engineering*, Vol. 23, No. 12, November 1997, pp. 736–743.

References: Briand, Lionel, Khaled El Emam, Dagmar Surmann, Isabella Wieczorek, and Katrina Maxwell, *An Assessment and Comparison of Common Software Cost Modeling Techniques*, Kaiserslautern, Germany: Fraunhofer Center for Empirical Software Engineering, ISERN technical report 98-27, 1998.

How the method works: Analogy-based estimation is used not only for size estimation but also for effort and schedule estimation. It is based on the notion that completed projects with characteristics similar to those of the proposed project can suggest the likely size. However, three issues need to be addressed: determining which projects are similar, selecting the appropriate attributes to determine similarity, and deciding how many similar projects must be collected before the size estimate can be determined from them. Some organizations use a similarity rule or algorithm to select similar projects. A panel of experts who understand the organization and the way that software supports it usually determines the similarity attributes. However, the initial selection of attributes may change, either as the attribute becomes unimportant or because the attributes are checked (using a historical database and statistical techniques such as classification tree analysis) to see which ones are the best predictors of size. It is difficult to know how many projects constitute a minimum number to support the analogy; that number may change as the number and type of similarity attributes change. The number also depends on the variability in the characteristics; low variability means that only a few projects are needed to judge similarity. Figure 3.4 shows how the process works.

Usually, the analogous projects are used to generate three estimates: "high," "low," and "most likely." The estimates can be derived using expert judgment, or they can be the result of applying machine learning techniques to the collection of similar projects. A simple rule

Figure 3.4
Using Analogies to Generate a Size Estimate

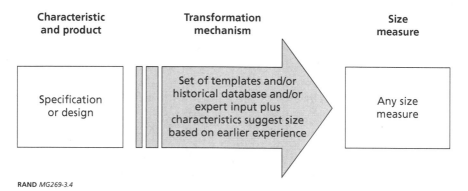

combines the three estimates into one. Typically, the rule assigns more weight to the most likely estimate, using a function such as

$$\text{Size} = \frac{1}{6}([\text{low}] + 4[\text{most\_likely}] + [\text{high}]) \qquad (3.3)$$

When to use the method: Analogies are useful in the very early stages of project definition, before items such as number of screens or transactions are well understood. Especially when an organization develops a product line or a series of similar products, analogies can consider already-known products as a baseline from which size estimates are derived. A historical database of information can help to reduce the uncertainty inherent in relying on expert judgment.

When not to use the method: When a project is very different from what has been developed before, analogies may not be appropriate. Sometimes it is tempting to then call on information from other organizations. However, Briand et al. (1998) point out that "Analogy-based models do not seem as robust when using data external to the organization for which the model is built." That is, analogies work best when they rely on an understanding of the organization at hand; it can be misleading to use data and anecdotes from outside organizations or from radically different projects.

Estimating from Unified Modeling Language Constructs

Source: Galorath, Daniel D., and Daniel V. Ferens, "A Software Model Based on Architecture," El Segundo, Calif.: Galorath Incorporated, informal working paper, n.d.

References: Galorath Incorporated, "Software Size Analysis for Integrated Logistics System-Supply (ILS-S)," El Segundo, Calif., Revised Report for Air Force Cost Analysis Agency, June 21, 2002. This report uses a UML-based estimate as a secondary source of size prediction.

A brief description of UML, including its constructs and uses, is in Chapter 6 of Shari Lawrence Pfleeger and Joanne Atlee, *Software Engineering: Theory and Practice*, 3rd ed., Upper Saddle River, N.J.: Prentice Hall, 2005.

How the method works: Unified Modeling Language (UML) is popular today for capturing requirements and for describing the overall architecture of a software-intensive system. One of the UML constructs is a use case, which graphically depicts the way in which a user will interact with the system to perform one function or one class of functions. Three aspects of use cases can be helpful as inputs to a size estimate: the number of use cases, the number of actors involved in each use case, and the number of scenarios. An *actor* is a person or system that interacts with the system under consideration; typically, there is one actor per use case, but sometimes there are more. A *scenario* is a potential outcome from using the software; the number of scenarios can range from one to thousands or millions, depending on the system and its complexity.

The philosophy behind a use case–based estimate is similar to that of function points: Each aspect is a significant driver of size. This similarity is evident in Figure 3.5. Thus, an experienced UML analyst can read a set of requirements and translate them into the likely number of use cases, actors, and scenarios. As with function points, different analysts can generate different estimates of the aspects. But, also as with function points, experience helps to reduce the variability across different analysts.

Figure 3.5
Generating a Size Estimate from Use Cases

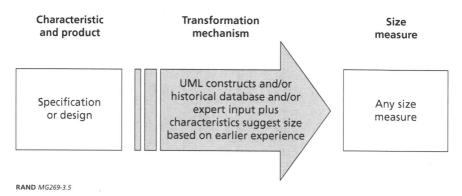

The Galorath procedure for using UML characteristics translates the size estimate into function points, using regression based on data sets from completed projects. Two of the inputs—use cases and actors—are first adjusted with weights according to their complexity (low, average, or high) as determined by the number of transactions or the user's interaction with the system. Then regression equations (based on historical data) are used to perform the translation to function points. (Note that, although Galorath does not attempt an extension, this general procedure can in fact be extended to translate to any size measure, if need be.)

When a historical database is not available, Galorath uses *genetic* algorithms (a technique used by biologists to deal with genetic mutations) and neural networks to adjust the weights, and a statistical technique called ensemble theory to do the translation.

The UML-based approach is not well evaluated in the literature, in part because it is new and in part because some of the techniques are proprietary.

When to use the method: This technique can be useful when the size estimate is required after a UML specification is done. It can also be used as a cross-check of another method; if the answers from both methods are similar, the analysts may have more confidence in the result.

When not to use the method: There is considerable risk in using this technique. It is relatively new and has not been well tested. It should be used only when the consequences of inaccuracy are minimal.

This chapter has described the variety of size-estimation techniques available to a cost analyst, including their pros and cons. Each technique is suitable only to certain situations, and each involves some risk in producing an accurate estimate. The next chapter examines the risks in more detail, building a checklist to assist cost analysts in choosing an appropriate technique and minimizing risk.

CHAPTER FOUR
Risk Checklist for Sizing Methods

Any size estimate involves making decisions about the inputs to the estimation process and about the process itself; the result is a size estimate as output. Each input has an associated uncertainty, and the size estimate produced has an associated degree of risk. The issues discussed in the preceding chapter, and the pros and cons related to them, can be viewed as risks to estimation. In this chapter, we explore in greater depth the risks and uncertainties, and we generate a check list of items an analyst can consider when creating or evaluating a size estimate.

Project managers and other decisionmakers who estimate software size are aware of many of the risks in the estimation process. Some are risks that they can control, but many others are risks over which they have little if any control. It is important to understand that the models in and of themselves cannot always mitigate these risks. As a result, model users and decisionmakers are sometimes discouraged to find that many size models are unable to produce a more accurate size estimate, even after repeated use with experienced developers and analysts. The key to dealing with this discouragement is to learn to manage the risk and anticipate the variation in estimates, rather than to deny that risk and variation exist or to repeatedly commission a new model or method.

We begin this chapter by exploring the major areas in which risks may occur within the size-estimation process. Then, we provide risk checklists to guide analysts and decisionmakers in their understanding of what causes the various risks, what symptoms of risk occurrence may exist, and what mitigation strategies may be taken.

Risks

Sources of risk in software size estimates derive from places where errors can be made in the estimation process. As shown in Figure 4.1, two elements of the process can be in error: the data and the estimation process. That is, one source of error is that there may be incorrect or incomplete data items, such as descriptions of how the software will be developed or notions of how the user will use the software system. Another source of error derives from correct data being using incorrectly, as when a computation is not complete or is

Figure 4.1
Relationships Among Uncertainties and Errors

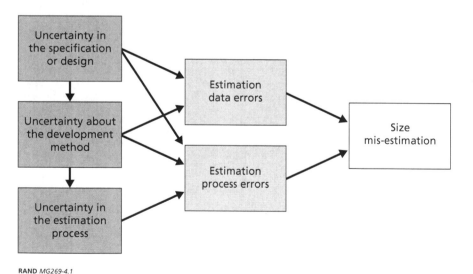

RAND MG269-4.1

applied inappropriately. But these errors themselves are derived from three kinds of uncertainty:

- in the specification or design
- about the development method
- in the estimation process.

While uncertainty does not invariably lead to error, it does greatly increase the chance that errors can occur, if not dealt with properly. Uncertainty in the specification and design is natural, especially when the size estimate is being made early in the development process to support a bid/no-bid decision. Here, the clients and developers are still negotiating, trying to determine what is needed. This kind of uncertainty also comes from difficulties in communicating needs, and from unrealistic expectations about capabilities afforded by new and unproven technologies (so that there is little documentation of effects).

Uncertainty about the development method comes from the general lack of understanding of cause and effect between software-development technologies and their resulting products. For example, we know that building prototypes helps to improve understanding of requirements and design trade-offs; therefore, we include prototyping in the development process. But for some sizing methods, the size estimate could include the size of the prototypes. Because the effect of evaluating the prototype is not known until it is built, it is impossible to know with any accuracy how large the final product will be. That is, prototypes are often used to explore feasibility of design or to determine whether a particular problem can be solved. If the prototype reveals that a design or problem is more complex than originally anticipated, more effort may be required than had originally been estimated.

Finally, uncertainty is inherent in the estimation process itself. Even when trained and experienced in particular estimation techniques, analysts often interpret the technique's instructions differently. Ratings of those characteristics that are included in evaluating function points or application points can vary slightly from one analyst to another; no two analysts will give exactly the same prediction.

Cost analysts must play a role in influencing these risks and uncertainties. To see how, we describe the variety of risks that might occur, the warning signs that the risk is present, and potential mitigation strategies that cost analysts can take or can direct the developers to take. If necessary, they can turn each of these items into a question or inquiry to be used as a means of finding out about the program.

To manage the risks in size estimation, cost analysts can review each size estimate to determine the presence of each type of risk. Looking for the risk entails three activities: knowing where to look, seeking signs that the risk is present, and understanding the steps that can be taken to address and manage the risk. Consequently, this section is organized according to three questions:

- What is the source of the risk?
- What are the uncertainties and indicators of risk?
- What steps can be taken to address these risks?

Using Figure 4.1 as a template, we use the three sources of uncertainty as entry points to the checklist.

The Specification or Design

The specification or design is often key to the accuracy of a size estimate. Especially when the estimate is produced early in the development process, there are risks associated with the uncertainty in the specification or design.

Risk: Problems in understanding the requirements or design.

Symptoms or warning signs: Especially when a system is groundbreaking, the organization commissioning the system may not know how to describe what it wants. Warning signs of uncertainty associated with the specification or design include repeated revision of the specification or design documents, the use of "TBD" or "TBS" (to be determined or supplied) throughout the documents, and incompleteness in important portions of the documents. Other symptoms of significant problems are ambiguity or conflict in the documents, or difficulty translating the requirements into design components or test plans.

Mitigation strategies: The uncertainty in the requirements and design can be reduced by holding requirements and design reviews, by prototyping the requirements and design, and by asking the test team to begin designing tests at the same time that designers are fleshing out detailed design from the requirements.

Risk: Incomplete or inconsistent requirements or design.

Symptoms or warning signs: Sometimes the organization specifying or designing a system assumes the availability or compatibility of certain portions of the system that is to be developed. For example, the requirements describe the reuse of software from another, previously built system, the integration of government-supplied or off-the-shelf software, or conformity to a specified standard (such as an interface). Or requirements in different parts of the specification conflict in some way. Warning signs include inability to determine a use for each subsystem described in the requirements, to understand when a feature or portion of the system is created, updated, or deleted, to understand how two features interact, or to determine the relationship between the user and the system.

Mitigation strategies: This type of uncertainty in the requirements and design can be reduced by developing use cases for the system, by holding requirements and design reviews, by prototyping the design and interfaces, and by asking the test team to begin designing tests at the same time that designers are fleshing out detailed design from the requirements.

The mitigation strategies for problems in understanding, as well as for incomplete/inconsistent requirements and design, force the developers to ask detailed, careful questions about the meaning and implication of each requirement or design component; then, problems surface early and are resolved well before implementation begins. A side benefit is that the requirements and design are of higher quality and lower uncertainty for estimation purposes.

The Development Method

The development method itself can introduce uncertainty in the estimation process. Well-known, well-understood development methods or techniques may involve little risk, but new technologies with unknown consequences can lead to inaccurate estimates. For example, reusing components may seem appealing, but the actual reuse may require more modification than originally thought; in some cases, it may be faster to design or code the components anew. Similarly, iterative or incremental development may seem appealing at first, but the design may make such development impossible. The Air Force's Integrated Logistics System (ILS-S) is an example of the incremental approach, which involved replacing pieces of an old system with new ones. However, the nature of the old design and code led to abandoning that approach and embracing new development.

Risk: Economies and diseconomies of scale.

Symptoms or warning signs: Sometimes, techniques that have good effects in the small can have bad effects in the large. For example, using formal methods to prove the correctness of requirements has been shown to find problems in requirements, but using formal methods on a large scale can be expensive, time-consuming, and sometimes infeasible. Symptoms of diseconomies of scale include inability to judge the effects of the candidate technology on the size of development and inability to decide which parts of the system should be subject to the technology (such as deciding which portions of the requirements should be proven correct using formal methods).

Mitigation strategies: It may be useful to decompose the system into subsystems and then do a size estimate for each subsystem. Such decomposition can be based on the work breakdown structure (WBS, a formal description of the tasks and their dependencies) or on functional subsystems, each of which will be developed in a different way.

Risk: Mismatch between the proposed development method and the estimation's assumed method.

Symptoms or warning signs: Many size-estimation methods assume that the system will be developed in a particular way. For example, the predictive object points method requires that the system be described in an object-oriented way; it may not be appropriate for procedural development methodologies. In general, if the estimation method is not matched to the development method, an inaccurate or misleading estimate can result. Warning signs include an inability to describe the system using the constructs of the estimation method, recognition that a significant contributor to the size is not accounted for in the estimation method, or difficulty deciding how to translate the characteristics of the development method into the parameters of the size-estimation technique.

Mitigation strategies: It can be useful to evaluate or enumerate the major determinants of size before selecting a size-estimation technique. Then, cost analysts can select the estimation technique that best captures the key size determinants.

The Estimation Process

The size-estimation process itself is the richest source of uncertainty in the estimate, because the accuracy of the estimate is so dependent on the way in which the process captures project characteristics that are related to size. Unlike other estimation approaches (such as effort- and schedule-estimation techniques), size is mostly dependent on understanding the constructs that underpin the software's designs. Whereas effort and schedule estimations introduce many human factors, such as variation in productivity or parallelism of effort, size estimation is more focused on the product than on the development process or the resources used to build the software.

Risk: Subjectivity in interpreting the adjustment factors.

Symptoms or warning signs: In sizing models, such as the function-point model, the adjustment factor is composed of several items, some of which can be interpreted differently, depending on the analyst's understanding, experience, and context. For example, an analyst experienced in estimating space-related systems may not be comfortable estimating the size and cost of weapon systems. Symptoms of uncertainty include difficulty in deciding whether to reflect a characteristic in one adjustment factor or in another, or counting the same type of function more than once.

Mitigation strategies: Where counting training exists, be sure that the analysts take it and ensure that the counting processes are consistent. Consistency can be checked periodically by asking analysts to generate estimates from the same set of requirements and discuss as a group the reasons for any discrepancies.

Risk: Lack of independence in the adjustment factors.

Symptoms or warning signs: In sizing models, such as the function-point model, the adjustment factor is composed of several items, some of which can be dependent on others. The dependence can lead to overcounting or double-counting the same things. Symptoms of uncertainty include difficulty in deciding whether to reflect a characteristic in one adjustment factor or in another, or counting the same type of function more than once.

Mitigation strategies: Look for independence in factors, and when dependence exists, moderate the factor measurement. (Note that moderation is not straightforward; it involves taking steps to prevent double-counting. Such steps may include reducing the value of several adjustment factors so that the combination of factors is not greater than it should be. Often, expert judgment is needed to make such changes.)

Risk: Values for adjustment factors are counterintuitive.

Symptoms or warning signs: In such sizing models as function points or COCOMO, which use a nominal size estimate that is then adjusted by descriptive factors, sometimes the adjustment factors seem to relate to an average or baseline project, but the actual values do not seem right. For example, in function points, a designation of "average" translates to 1.07 in the adjustment factor, but analysts may assume that 1.0 is "average" across the board. If the adjustment factors are not used properly or are misinterpreted, over- or under-estimation can result.

Mitigation strategies: Focus on the actual values, not the English-language descriptions of them. It may also be useful to know which models have non-intuitive definitions of "average," and to keep a chart of their definitions.

Risk: Adjustment factors do not seem relevant to the current project.

Symptoms or warning signs: In such sizing models as function points or COCOMO, which use a nominal size estimate that is then adjusted by descriptive factors, the adjustment factors may be based on an application area or type of development that is not the same as what is proposed for the current project. Symptoms include having trouble deciding which rating to give a factor, because the factor seems out of place. At the same time, the factors may appear not to be addressing critical characteristics of the project. If the adjustment factors do not relate to the project, the size estimate may not reflect an important element and thus be too large or too small.

Mitigation strategies: Create a historical database of projects and use factors from similar projects to describe the current project. If necessary, consider defining new adjustment factors or possibly using a different (more relevant) model.

Risk: Rater bias.

Symptoms or warning signs: Each analyst brings to the estimation process his or her own experiences and biases. These biases can influence the way in which the estimation steps are interpreted and the estimation process is applied. As a result, misinterpretation and misunderstanding can lead to errors in estimation. Warning signs include disregarding some adjustment factors, inability to understand the variation in a set of similar projects, and insistence that the process rules be bent to accommodate a system feature.

Mitigation strategies: Have two or three analysts generate size estimates from the same specification or design; then, compare the results and bring the analysts to consensus on one value or interval. Alternatively, use several estimation techniques on one specification or design; then, justify the use of one of the estimates or produce a weighted combination of the several techniques as a single estimate. Retraining may also be in order, to remind analysts of the appropriate ways of applying the estimation techniques.

Risk: Inter-rater disagreements.

Symptoms or warning signs: It is always helpful to obtain estimates from several analysts, so that, as described above, a dramatic difference in estimates can make visible an analyst's misunderstanding or bias. But, sometimes, the inter-rater disagreements also highlight inherent ambiguities in the specification or design. In these cases, even when using the same technique, multiple analysts arrive at very different estimates. Warning symptoms include inability of the analysts to agree on input values, inability of the analysts to agree on which model is most appropriate to apply, or heated arguments about the estimation process's steps.

Mitigation strategies: The strategies to mitigate inter-rater disagreements include the same strategies employed to mitigate rater bias. In addition, the specification should be reviewed carefully, to identify inherent ambiguities or conflicts.

Risk: Inappropriate use of measurement.

Symptoms or warning signs: Underlying every estimation technique is the notion of how characteristics of the system are to be measured and the way the system is to be developed. The measurement is subject to the rules of measurement theory, including the idea that each measurement belongs to a particular measurement scale. For example, nominal measures are those that belong to unordered categories, such as type of programming language. Other scales include ordinal (where the categories of measures, such as error severity, can be ranked) and ratio (where the measurements, such as lines of code, can be added and subtracted). (More information about measurement scales and measurement theory can be found in Fenton and Pfleeger [1996].) When measurement is used inappropriately, errors can be introduced in the size estimate. For example, multiplying adjustment factors is appropriate only when the factors are independent; there is some question of whether the adjustments to function points or COCOMO are appropriate, for instance. Symptoms of inappropriate measurement include difficulty in using arithmetic operations on measurements, in combining measurements or distributions, or in generating adjustment factors or size estimates that seem counterintuitive.

Mitigation strategies: Identify the measurement scale for each input to the estimation process. Each measurement scale has associated with it a permitted set of transformations, including arithmetic operators. Check to see that the operations required by the estimation process are permitted for the measurements under scrutiny.

CHAPTER FIVE

Checklist for Reviewing Size-Estimation Risk

The warning signs and suggested mitigation strategies in Chapter Four can be reorganized as a checklist of steps to take when evaluating a size estimate. Using this checklist, an analyst can ask questions about the sizing-method selection, the project itself, and the application of the sizing method. When necessary, the analyst can then take the recommended actions to help characterize and manage the risks inherent in creating and using the size estimate.

1. Sizing-Method Selection

Is the selected sizing method appropriate, given the project characteristics?

Action: Describe each of the following project characteristics:

- life-cycle phase
- status and form of the system description/documentation
- revolutionary versus evolutionary nature of the system (determined in part by the existence of a predecessor system or idea)
- existence of similar systems
- system application or domain (e.g., data processing, transaction, real-time command and control).

Then, refer to Chapter Three, "When to Use" and "When Not to Use," for the given sizing method.

Is the selected sizing method appropriate, given the intended use of the size estimate?

Action: Describe the intended use of the estimate in terms of the following questions:

- Will it be used to support a new cost/size estimate?
- Will it update an existing cost/size estimate?
- Will it be used to measure progress or productivity?
- Will it be used to identify cost drivers?
- Will it be used to conduct a trade-off analysis?

Then, evaluate whether the chosen method will yield an output consistent with the intended use. Review "When to Use a Sizing Method" and "Issue: Tracking Changes and Progress Over Time," in Chapter Two, to help determine the appropriateness of the method for its intended use.

Is the selected sizing method appropriate, given the proposed development method?

Action: Review the section "Risk: Mismatch between the proposed development method and the estimation's assumed method," in Chapter Four, to determine whether the method is being used as an appropriate development method.

2. Project/System Assessment

Are the system concepts and functions well defined?

Action: Review the section "Risk: Problems in understanding the requirements or design," in Chapter Four.

Is the system architecture (to include interfaces) complete?

Action: Review the section "Risk: Incomplete or inconsistent requirements or design," in Chapter Four.

Does the size of the system warrant decomposition and estimation of the elements?

Action: Review the section "Risk: Economies and diseconomies of scale," in Chapter Four.

3. Sizing-Method Application

Was a guide or standard used in generating the estimate, to ensure consistency (particularly across multiple estimating organizations)?

Action: Review the discussions of the disadvantages in "Issue: Counting physical objects" and "Issue: Counting notional constructs," in Chapter Two.

Is the analyst adequately trained or experienced in using notional constructs (function points, object points, etc.)?

Action: Review the discussion of the disadvantages of "Counting notional constructs," in Chapter Two.

What was done to minimize the uncertainty introduced by the use of adjustment factors?

Action: Review the risks addressed in Chapter Four as "Subjectivity and lack of independence in the adjustment factors," "Values for adjustment factors are counterintuitive," and "Adjustment factors do not seem relevant to current project."

What was done to minimize the uncertainty introduced by mis-measurement or misuse of the measure for system characteristics?

Action: Review the "Risk: Inappropriate use of measurement" subsection, in Chapter Four.

If a single analyst developed the estimate, what steps were taken to minimize bias by the analyst?

Action: Review the risk discussed in "Rater bias," in Chapter Four.

If multiple analysts developed the estimate, what steps were taken to reach agreement?

Action: Review the risk discussed in the "Inter-rater bias" subsection of Chapter Four.

Was the estimate translated from one size measure to another?

Action: If so, review the discussion of the disadvantages of "Counting notional constructs," in Chapter Two, and inquire about how the translation was accomplished.

Was it necessary to calibrate or tune the method to fit the development?

Action: Review the disadvantages of "Lack of Empirical Evidence" and the discussion of "Calibration," in Chapter Two.

How were previous experience and knowledge (such as a historical database) used to develop the size estimate?

Action: Review the issue of "Using Past Project Experience and Information," in Chapter Two.

What is the risk assessment for the estimate? That is, how is the risk expressed as an interval or distribution?

Action: Review the "Risks" section of Chapter Four and inquire about how the risk was captured and quantified. Determine the confidence interval, and assess whether the confidence limits are realistic.

Does the size estimate rely on one or more methods?

Action: If so, review how the component estimates were developed and integrated.

Other questions can be posed during the estimation process or when the resulting estimate is being assessed:

- What assumptions were used to generate the estimate? Are any of the assumptions different from the types of assumptions covered in the above checklist?

- If the estimate assumes that some part of the system will be reused from past systems, what assumptions were made regarding any effort required to reuse the requirements, design, code, or tests (sometimes referred to as reuse percentages)?
- If the estimate assumes reuse of commercial off-the-shelf software, how familiar are the developers with the items to be reused? Does the estimate include a learning curve for understanding the targeted items before they are adapted for use in the proposed system?
- Does the analyst anticipate any growth in the size? When and why? What factors are most likely to contribute to growth if it occurs?
- Is there a configuration-managed software development plan (that is, a plan to manage the various versions and releases of the software as it evolves) and, if so, how was configuration management considered in generating the size estimate?
- Does the size estimate address the effort required for integration (in large multi site/multi team projects)?

This checklist can form the skeleton of an evolving list of questions asked by cost analysts. That is, as analysts learn more about estimation techniques and how they are used, and about how different organizations develop software, they can expand the questions to address areas in which the estimates have high degrees of uncertainty or inaccuracy.

The checklist framework assists the analyst in understanding the genesis of a size estimate and in performing a reality check. At the same time, it helps to identify the risks inherent in estimating size, thereby enabling the project participants to manage the risks, not only in the estimation process but also during software development and maintenance.

CHAPTER SIX

Approaches to Cost Estimation

Sizing is only one aspect of estimating how much effort will be involved in developing, delivering, and maintaining software. In this chapter, we turn our attention to the issues involved in producing useful, accurate cost estimates.

Cost estimation is as much an art as a science. Estimating the cost of a proposed piece of software involves many steps, including an assessment of how the software requirements are likely to be implemented in design and code. This estimation process depends not only on using one or more estimation models but also on applying the experience and judgment of the analyst to selecting an appropriate model, determining the input values, and evaluating the reasonableness of the result.

As noted in Chapter One, software size estimation is critical to providing a credible software cost estimate. Existing models usually base their effort predictions on two elements: the size of the software to be developed and the environment (the tools, resources, and development techniques) in which it is developed. In most cases, the estimation risk—that is, the possibility that the cost estimate will be far from the actual software cost—depends more on accurate size estimates than on any other cost-related parameter, including the development environment. (For example, Boehm et al. [2000] notes that "the most significant input to the COCOMO II model is Size.") That is, the environment is generally used to generate adjustments to the initial size-derived effort estimate, by using multipliers that reflect environmental characteristics. Although, historically, size has represented the magnitude of the problem being solved by the software, some recent estimation models use complexity or functionality to represent the magnitude; these models attempt to overcome some of the problems inherent in trying to know the size early in the development.

Other factors incorporated in adjusting the initial estimate often include the application domain, the experience of the developers, the complexity of the problem and its solution, the interaction among different developer sites, and more. Each of these factors has an associated degree of uncertainty; it is impossible to know with absolute certainty how the factors will influence the outcome, or even whether the factors will change over the course of development. Thus, it is important that software estimation be done as consistently and accurately as possible while taking into account the uncertainties inherent in estimation.

Typically, software is a significant portion of the development effort of a modern weapon or information technology system, making its cost significant, too. The risks involved in estimating software costs will necessarily affect the other costs associated with the system, including hardware costs and maintenance costs. However, for the purposes of this document, we consider the software costs in isolation; we leave it to the cost analyst to determine how the uncertainties in software costs relate to the costs of hardware, integration, and maintenance.

Using Cost Estimates

Cost estimates for software development and maintenance activities are frequently associated with decisions about affordability, investment, and value. *Affordability* includes not only the costs necessary to accomplish the development but also those costs that address training, repair, and upgrades over the intended system's life cycle. *Investment* decisions consider whether the associated costs will yield a specific capability within the time and resources available. *Value* may consider whether other options can provide a more affordable or less risky investment to achieve the desired capability.

Thus, the way in which a cost estimate is used often depends on the types of decisions that need to be made, when they are needed, and who is making them. In particular, we can view a cost estimate from the perspective of the system's buyer, developer, or user, as well as from the perspective of a researcher who is trying to analyze how well a model or technique meets intended needs. The different uses of cost estimates suggest that the inherent risks differ, based on perspective and need. Thus, the relationship of risk to cost estimation can be understood only with a concomitant understanding of how estimation is performed.

Buyers
The buyer commissions or contracts with the developer to build the software system. For the buyer, a cost estimate can be useful for

- analyzing alternative means to fulfill the buyer's need
- budgeting or planning for the new system, an upgrade, or maintenance
- forecasting life-cycle costs
- evaluating alternative proposals for new development, upgrades, or maintenance.

Developers
Developers work on behalf of the buyer, a user, or themselves (or their organizations) to build a software system. The developers use cost estimates to

- analyze alternative development strategies
- prepare proposals for a development, upgrade, or maintenance
- budget or plan resources (people and time) to execute a development, upgrade, or maintenance
- monitor resources and productivity to manage a development, upgrade, or maintenance.

Users

Users employ the completed or evolving system to accomplish a task or mission. If there is no separate purchasing organization, the user may, in fact, be the same as the buyer. If a separate purchasing organization exists, the user has other needs for a cost estimate. In particular, the estimate gives the user a sense of how much effort is involved in creating new functionality or changing existing functionality. The estimate also enables the user to understand the cost of improving system performance or security.

Researchers

Researchers are often one level removed from the buyers, developers, and users. They investigate questions about estimation models (and their inputs and outputs) to help improve the overall estimation process. They may collect and analyze data to help quantify the nature of a problem and to build models that will enhance the estimation process.

Cost-Estimation Approaches

It is helpful to review the several different approaches that a cost analyst can take in producing a cost estimate, to better develop a sense of where risks lay in the estimation process.

There are many ways to approach estimation, from informal methods that rely heavily on expertise and experience, to very formal parametric methods based on formulas derived from past performance. In addition, there are hybrid methods that borrow concepts from a variety of approaches. In this section, we provide an overview of several widely recognized methods for estimating software costs. For each one, we describe how it works, including its advantages and disadvantages. These descriptions represent the canonical techniques. Practice and the literature often recommend that several estimation methods be used in concert (when possible) to mitigate the bias, shortcomings, or risks of using a single method.

1. Expert Judgment Method

How it works: Human experts provide cost and schedule estimates based on their experience. Usually, they have knowledge of similar development efforts, and the degree of similarity is relative to their understanding of the proposed project. In some sense, we can think of expert judgment as an educated guess about the effort to be expended to develop an entire project or a portion of it. However, the guess is a sophisticated judgment supported by a variety of tools to assist the analysts in leveraging what they know. For example, they may tap a database of historical information from past projects to help them understand where the current project fits in. Modeling tools based on statistical or artificial-intelligence techniques can assist analysts in finding a similar project or in distinguishing one project from another. Usually, the estimate is not generated from a high-level description of what the system will do. Instead, it is derived from either a top-down or a bottom-up analysis of the proposed system's size and functionality. Often, the experts are asked to make three predictions: a pessimistic (high) one, an optimistic (low) one, and a most-likely guess. The final estimate of effort, $\hat{E}$, is the mean of the beta probability distribution, defined as

$$\hat{E} = \frac{1}{6}([\text{low}]+4[\text{most\_likely}]+[\text{high}]) \qquad (6.1)$$

More-structured applications of expert judgment can employ methods such as the Delphi Technique, developed by the RAND Corporation in 1948. A group of experts is asked to make individual predictions secretly. Then, the average estimate is calculated and presented to the group, and the experts are given the opportunity to revise their estimates, if they so wish. The process repeats until no expert wants to change her or his estimate.

Advantages: Human experts can calibrate previous experiences and data by considering the differences (e.g., application, development environment, technologies, languages, organization) between previous projects and the proposed project.

Disadvantages: The main disadvantage is that the estimate is heavily dependent upon the judgment of the expert and, therefore, may be subjective. There may be very limited visibility into the process and factors that the expert considered in developing the estimate, thus making the estimate itself difficult to accept and even more difficult to document appropriately. This technique may be particularly troublesome for organizations without groups of software engineering experts. When experts rely on memories of previous projects, rather than on historical databases, there is little documentation available to verify that the estimate is reasonable.

Even when it is known and clear how one project differs from another, completed project, it is not always apparent how the differences affect the cost. A proportional-cost strategy, wherein interpolation or extrapolation is used to estimate the new project from historical data, is unreliable because project costs are not necessarily linear: two people cannot produce code twice as fast as one. Extra time may be needed for coordination and communication or to accommodate for differences in ability, interest, and experience. For example, in a classic software engineering study, Sackman, Erikson, and Grant (1968) found that the ratio between the best and worst performance on productivity measurements averaged ten to one, and there was no easily definable relationship between the experience of programmers and their performance. Such dramatic variation in productivity adds significant uncertainty to any estimate of effort.

Usage: Because of its high degree of uncertainty, this method usually complements other methods. It is most useful when experts have relevant experience, knowledge, or data from previous projects and an understanding of the proposed project. This method should not be used if there are aspects of the project that are completely new to the analysts performing the estimation. Since it requires few constructs or detailed parameters for its use, expert judgment is frequently used early in the project life cycle, particularly before the detailed design or requirements are fully specified.

2. Analogy Method

How it works: Estimation by analogy is similar to expert judgment in that it relies on a comparison and adjustment between a previous project and the proposed project. It draws heavily on historical data from previously completed and similar projects on which project development information is known. It also requires the use of expert opinion to adjust the actual costs or effort of the completed project to account for differences between it and the proposed project. This technique can be applied at the system or component level and may employ tools such as historical databases and parametric strategies.

Advantages: This method relies on data from actual projects, thereby avoiding expert judgment's reliance on recall. It also avoids the complexity of parametric/algorithmic models. Templates can be built to characterize different kinds of projects or project attributes, to explicitly account for differences between previous projects and the proposed project. Tools, such as Bournemouth University's ANGEL (Shepperd and Schofield, 1997), can be used to support the estimation.

Disadvantages: Because this method depends on expert judgment to account for differences and to extrapolate from a previous project to the current project, it can be challenging and subjective. For example, two projects that may seem similar may indeed be different in a critical way (just as a runner who runs a four-minute mile cannot run a marathon in under two hours). Moreover, the uncertainty in assessing similarity and difference means that two different analysts may have significantly different views and eventual estimates. This difficulty can be mitigated by using historical data, which in turn requires maintaining and using a database of templates or project data.

Usage: As with expert judgment, this method is not suitable when the estimation analysts have neither experience nor data for similar projects. Similarly, the method is not useful when some aspect of the proposed system is dramatically different in some way from most of the other projects in the database or in the analysts' experience. However, analogies may be useful when estimates are needed from sparse, high-level system descriptions, particularly before detailed design or requirements are fully specified.

3. Parametric/Algorithmic Method

How it works: Parametric or algorithmic methods are models that use cost-estimating relationships (CERs) to associate system characteristics with the estimates of effort and duration. The CERs are based on research and analysis of historical data. In particular, they often use some type of regression analysis to determine relationships between effort and some system attribute, such as number of users, number of transactions, or required reliability.

A regression analysis is a statistical technique that uses historical data of estimated values and actual results. If the estimated and actual values are plotted on a graph so that the estimated values are on the *x*-axis and the actual values are on the *y*-axis, all the historical data sit on the 45-degree line between the *x*- and *y*-axes in the ideal situation, as shown in Figure 6.1a. However, in the more typical case, the data points represented by (estimates, actuals) form a cluster of points. A *linear regression analysis* fits a line among the points in order to minimize the sum of the distances from each point to the line.

Figure 6.1
(a) The Ideal Case, in Which Estimated Values Are Equal to Actual Values; and (b) the Typical Case, in Which Estimated Values Differ from Actual Values (the line represents a regression line fitted to the data points)

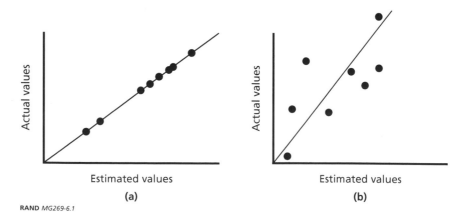

RAND *MG269-6.1*

We say that the regression "fits" a line among the points, as shown in Figure 6.1b. This line has an equation, and that equation is then used to estimate the next value. That is, the line based on historical data is used to predict the behavior of the project; the assumption is that the new project has characteristics similar to those of past projects, and thus will have similar behavior.

More-sophisticated regression models can be developed using the same philosophy. Sometimes, the model fits a curve instead of a line to the points; this is called *nonlinear regression*. Often, the model takes into account many of the characteristics of a project, then develops a regression equation based on the relationship between the characteristics and the actual effort, as determined from historical data. That is, instead of having the estimated values on the x-axis, the x-axis represents a variety of project characteristics (often called *cost factors*) that can affect the effort.

The method is called *parametric* because it displays effort as the dependent variable and some set of attributes—the cost factors—as independent variables. The algorithm is the rule, formula, or set of rules that derives the cost estimate from the parameters. Various models differ not only in the expression of the relationships among cost factors but also in the choice of factors included in the model.

Ideally, a parametric or algorithmic model should be useful no matter what development paradigm, tool, or implementation language is employed. This universal applicability allows the model to be used with many development processes, such as waterfall, evolutionary, or transformational development.[5] Similarly, a good model can

---

[5] The *waterfall development process* involves a series of sequential steps, whereby each step must be completed before the next one can begin. By contrast, *evolutionary processes*, including incremental or spiral development, employ a recurring, or cyclic, set of steps; when uncertainty arises in a given step, the developers can return to previous steps to reduce the uncertainty before proceeding with system development. *Transformational processes* apply (usually automated) formal processes to transform the output of one step to input for the next step; for example, a transformation applied to a set of requirements yields a preliminary design. In turn, the design is transformed to code. The transformations are usually accomplished by writing the input in a formal language, then applying an automated process, much as one applies a compiler to a higher-level language to get executable code.

be applied to a variety of design techniques, such as functional decomposition or object-oriented approaches.

However, the reality is quite different. Because many elements of a given cost-estimation model reflect the way the software will be developed, it is essential to ensure that the chosen model reflects the underlying development process. For example, in an incremental development approach (in which successive development efforts build on the results of prior development efforts, expanding functionality with each increment), it may be necessary to take extra precautions to consider the total development context. In this sample case, the estimated effort must include the work involved in integrating the previous system with the new functionality. Since many effort-estimation models assume one pass through the life cycle to generate all functionality, such models would be inappropriate for incremental development. A similar analysis is needed for understanding the effort involved in reusing or modifying components.

As noted above, models can be linear or nonlinear. A linear estimation model produces an equation of the form

$$E = c_0 + \sum_{i=1}^{n} c_i x_i \qquad (6.2)$$

and a nonlinear model is of the form

$$E = c_0 + \sum_{i=1}^{n} c_i x_i^{d_i} \qquad (6.3)$$

[d_i is the exponent of x_i] where E represents effort (usually in person-days), and c_i and d_i are constants derived from a historical database. The constants do not represent any project characteristics. Rather, they are derived using regression so that they describe the line or curve that best fits the data points through which the line or curve passes. Each variable x_i represents an attribute of the system or system-development process that affects the cost (such as the level of developer expertise or the degree to which reuse will affect the project). For the nonlinear model, in which the size of the project is considered to be the most important factor in the effort equation, the size parameter can be factored out and expressed separately. Then, the model can be rewritten to reflect the use of size as the primary cost factor,

$$E = (a + bS^c)m(\mathbf{X}) \tag{6.4}$$

where S is the estimated size of the system, and a, b, and c are regression-derived constants (that describe the shape of the curve fitted through the data points). $\mathbf{X}$ is a vector of cost factors xi through xn; that is, it represents n different characteristics of the project, such as level of experience of the development team, level of reuse, complexity of the problem to be solved, and so on. m is a functional adjustment based on these factors. Thus, effort is expressed as a function of size and is then adjusted by other mitigating factors. The adjustment can be a nonlinear function of several variables, and it may not be easily analyzed using regression. Thus, it is sometimes useful to derive the effort equation using only a baseline estimate for a nominal amount of effort in terms of lines of code:

$$E = a + bS^c \tag{6.5}$$

Advantages: Parametric or algorithmic models require calibration. That is, their parameters and adjustment factors are derived from sets of data describing completed projects. However, a particular organization must apply the same derivation techniques to its own data, rather than relying on data from other, likely less-relevant, organizations that may have been supplied in the research paper or tool invoking the model. Calibration forces the model to reflect the specific development environments and conditions experienced by the analysts who are about to use it; in turn, the model is usually more accurate, more repeatable, and less subjective.

Disadvantages: Parametric models are appealing to engineers, because they seem to provide a recipe for generating a scientifically based estimate. However, they are rife with problems:

- First, the models often incorporate large sets of attributes, which forces organizations to track large amounts of data to supply to the models.
- Second, analysts must understand not only the meaning of all the attributes but also the dependencies among them. A lack of such understanding can lead to widely varying estimates from different analysts.
- Third, calibration can involve significant effort, especially when large numbers of parameters require large volumes of project information to enable the database to describe all possible combinations of parameters.
- Fourth, CERs based on a particular application or development environment may require rederivation if the policies or environments change. At the same time, recalibration may be required when changes make the data or model used to develop the original CERs obsolete. For example, if the existing historical databases reflect projects that are designed and developed using significantly different methods (say, object-oriented versus functional decomposition) from the ones to be used in the proposed project, then the model parameters (as estimated by the historical data) may not appropriately reflect the real determinants of cost. Similarly, if the model is based on a development process that is no longer in use, the model must be reworked.

An additional problem derives from the fact that a size estimate is the major underlying contributor to the effort value. As noted earlier in this report, size estimates are subject to errors because they are difficult to develop with any certainty early in the development process. A good size estimate depends on many things, including the analyst's knowledge of the system, the constructs used to describe the system design and functionality, the extent to which the system will include new, reused, or modified components, and even the selection and application of an appropriate size-estimation method. Significant size errors will likely overshadow other sources of error, such as minor attribute changes, in the effort estimate.

Usage: Parametric or algorithmic models can be used with success as long as their use is constrained by several factors:

- First, it is important to understand the environment in which a given model is intended to be applied. This environment involves not only the development process on which the model is based but also the historical data from which the parameters and coefficients are derived. The model must be calibrated using data from appropriate situations and projects; otherwise, its results are suspect.
- Similarly, the model's CERs must be well understood before use. In particular, the type of regression and the degree of interpolation or extrapolation must be appropriate for the type of prediction being made. For example, if the model is derived from projects ranging in size from 1,000 to 10,000 lines of code, it is inappropriate to use it for estimating projects whose size is in the millions of lines of code.
- Third, use of the model must take into account the degree of uncertainty related to estimated size. Since size is usually the largest contributing factor in estimating the effort, and since accurately determining size is challenging, the size estimate should incorporate a confidence interval. This bounding of the size estimate can be explicit (where models incorporate a likely size distribution) or implicit (where the model is exercised repeatedly on representative points within the likely size distribution). The recognition of uncertainty in this way is particularly important for early life-cycle estimates when the requirements are not well defined or understood; however, it can be beneficial even as more is learned about the system as development progresses. Hancock (1982) points out the key difficulty in tracking size throughout development:

> As the system design requirements increase in difficulty and quantity, the number of related interactive items to be considered increases at some greater rate, thus intensifying the difficulty in developing a good estimate.

4. Bottom-Up/Work Breakdown Structure Method

How it works: The bottom-up method begins by decomposing a project into smaller elements, which are then estimated separately. All of these elements combined are often called a work breakdown structure. Individual-element estimates may be accomplished by a variety of estimating methods and are subject to the benefits and challenges of those methods. The individual estimates are then combined to produce a total estimate for the project.

Advantages: The bottom-up estimation process involves two steps: decomposition and integration. Performing those steps to form a consolidated estimate may make explicit many systems-level tasks, such as integration, documentation, project control, and configuration management; these tasks are sometimes ignored in other estimating methods (National Aeronautics and Space Administration [NASA], 2002). An additional advantage is that the work breakdown approach is often used with other engineering tasks, especially those related to hardware. Therefore, a bottom-up estimate can easily be integrated with other estimates to form a system cost estimate. For example, expert judgment may be applied to some elements of the system, and parametric methods can be used for others. In this way, elements can be matched with the most appropriate estimating techniques.

Disadvantages: This method is very resource-intensive. It requires an extensive knowledge not only of what the software will do but also of what staff roles will be assigned and what management approaches will be used (so that the tasks reflect these choices). Such information may not be known with any certainty early in the project, such as when bid/no-bid decisions must be made. In addition, the bottom-up method incorporates the disadvantages of any estimation methods selected to be used on various system elements. For example, if a parametric technique is chosen for estimating effort on a subsystem, the disadvantages of that technique must be considered. Another disadvantage of the bottom-up method is that some work, effort, or costs may be omitted inadvertently (because an analyst looking only at a small portion of a system may not be sensitive to the effort needed to integrate that portion with other system parts), whereas a parametric or other higher-level method tends to capture all the costs of the entire effort.

Usage: This method can be used when experts with detailed experience, knowledge, or data of the decomposed project elements are available. Because a bottom-up approach can take more time, it should be used only when time is available to construct the estimate. This method may be difficult to apply early in the project life cycle, particularly before an architecture or design would suggest how the decomposition might be done.

5. Top-Down Method

How it works: Similar in philosophy to the bottom-up method, a top-down estimate is derived by decomposing a project into lower-level elements or life-cycle phases. However, the effort estimate for each element is based on general project characteristics, rather than on detailed functional or design characteristics. Individual-element estimates are likely to be accomplished by analogy or expert judgment and are subject to the benefits and challenges of those techniques. The individual estimates are combined to develop a total estimate for the project.

Advantages: The top-down estimation process involves the same two steps as the bottom-up process—decomposition and integration; therefore, it has the same advantages as described for the bottom-up process.

Disadvantages: Although this method may seem faster and easier than other approaches, it may be less accurate because an analyst can easily overlook lower-level details or significant cost drivers that are made visible by other estimating techniques. Moreover, the limited detail makes the estimate difficult to document or verify, or to compare with more-detailed estimates.

Usage: This method can be used when experts with detailed experience, knowledge, or data of the decomposed project elements are available. This method may be difficult to apply early in the project life cycle, particularly before an architecture or design would suggest how the decomposition might be done.

Historical Databases to Support Estimation

It is important to note that each of the estimation approaches is enhanced by the existence and use of a historical database of project information. Not only can models be derived from such data, but the data are also essential for calibrating models, suggesting confidence levels, supporting expert judgments and analogies, and assisting any reality check of an estimate supplied to another source.

However, historical databases are like good hygiene: Everyone acknowledges that they are good to have, but not everyone follows through with careful practice. It takes time and effort to define the appropriate data elements, build a repository, gather and verify data, provide an effective interface to enable analysts to retrieve appropriate data, and use those data to build and calibrate models. In addition, the data may be proprietary or difficult to obtain by those maintaining the database. The costs related to the care and feeding of historical databases must be compared with the cost of generating poor estimates. In almost every case, the investment in historical data is well worth it (Boehm et al., 2000).

CHAPTER SEVEN

Risks in Cost Estimation

The risks in estimating size obviously affect the cost estimates, too. But there are additional risks in cost estimation, each of which is related to some kind of uncertainty. Indeed, we have noted repeatedly how uncertainty is inherent in many different steps of the estimation process. In this chapter, we view estimation in its larger context—that is, beyond size—to describe the sources of cost-estimation uncertainty, offering suggestions on using this knowledge to reduce risks in the cost-estimation process. The overarching message is that risk occurs in many different places throughout a project's life cycle, not just in size and not just in one step in the development process. Every time a decision is made, whether at the micro-level (such as how to design a particular module) or at the macro-level (such as which software architecture to employ), an element of uncertainty is introduced into the estimation process.

Uncertainty is further aggravated when cost estimates must be made very early in the project's life cycle. For a new project, the estimate's parameters (on which much of the effort estimate depends) must be measured or assessed at or near the very beginning of a project, before the actual software is written and, often, before the requirements are finalized. Historical databases of project information (including size and other project descriptors) can be used to reduce risk. For projects that have already started, some of the software may already be written, but additions, changes, and deletions are needed.

After a project starts, some risks occur that decisionmakers can control, but there are many others over which they have little if any control. Models in and of themselves are often unable to mitigate such risks.

This chapter discusses the major areas in which risks may occur within the cost-estimation process and provides risk checklists to guide the model user or decisionmaker in understanding what causes the various risks, what symptoms of risk occurrence exist, and what mitigation strategies may be taken.

Sources of Risk and Error

What are the sources of error in software cost and schedule estimates? Much as with sizing error, error is introduced into the data and the estimation process as a function of three types of uncertainty: in the system definition, in the system development, and in the estimation method. Figure 7.1 shows how these uncertainties contribute to risks that may lead to errors in software size and cost estimation.

Figure 7.1
How Uncertainties in Critical Components of a Software Project Lead to Risks That May Affect Cost- or Schedule-Estimation Accuracy

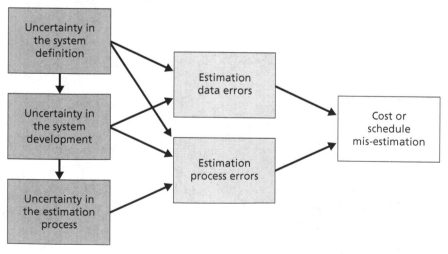

RAND *MG269-7.1*

These three components, and a cost analyst's role in influencing risks and uncertainties within them, are described below. Included with each description is a sample of the risks that might occur within each component, warning signs that the risk is present, and potential mitigation strategies. A cost analyst can turn each of these items into a question or inquiry to raise and clarify issues, thereby helping to reduce uncertainty and risk.

1. System Definition

Uncertainties regarding the required functionality or performance of the system affect both the accuracy of the effort estimate (particularly the estimated size) and the adjustment factors (such as likely complexity or data structures). These uncertainties can translate into erroneous inputs for the estimation data or difficulty understanding the role of system development, as shown by the arrows in Figure 7.1. For instance, if a new algorithm must be implemented and the performance of that algorithm has not been demonstrated previously in a comparable context, then there may be uncertainty about the effort required to satisfactorily develop this capability.

Unfortunately, cost analysts may have little influence in rectifying these uncertainties, since resolution is the responsibility of the client and developer. The cost analyst must judge how significant these uncertainties are and account for them in selecting estimation data or in reporting the estimate (for example, by specifying confidence intervals around the estimate).

What are the uncertainties and indicators of risk?

1. The problem is not sufficiently well defined. Symptoms may include the following:

   - Different people have different interpretations of what is needed.

- Significant portions or key parameters of the specification remain uncertain, with placeholders such as "TBD," "TBR," or "TBS."[6]
- The specification is thrashing. That is, the list that specifies what the system should do (and how well it should be done, in terms of performance, security, etc.) keeps changing. Sometimes these changes are healthy, as when prototypes give buyers and users a better sense of what is needed. But sometimes the revisions provide more heat than light; the rate of revisions (that is, the number of modifications over time) is not decreasing, and there seems to be no convergence on a set of requirements that all can agree to.
- The specification review process resulted in significant unresolved comments.
- There is inconsistency in the understanding of a project's size and needs, or there are changing conceptions of what the project will do.

2. The system use is not well understood. Symptoms include

- The concept of operations is incomplete, inconsistent, ambiguous, or does not exist.

3. The system is pushing the limits of technology. Evidence that this is happening includes

- Key requirements or functions are included in the program risk plan.

- Critical technologies have not been proven.

---

[6] D—determined, R—resolved, S—supplied. In any specification, there are likely to be some elements designated as yet to be determined, resolved, or supplied. Whether or not these placeholders are a problem depends on whether their number is decreasing, increasing, or staying constant over time (and possibly how fast this is happening). For example, placeholders may be desirable when feasibility is yet to be decided; in this case, more detail is expected in the specification as concepts are explored and clarified. Moreover, the significance of a placeholder may depend on where it occurs in the specification and how much of the rest of the system depends on it.

What steps can be taken to address these risks?

- Use ranges for size and effort, rather than single values.
- Conduct several estimates over time. Then determine whether the system definition is converging over time.
- Review program documentation, such as the system specification history, risk management plans, and operational concepts, to identify gaps and inconsistencies.
- Challenge data (both the nominal size and effort inputs and the adjustment factors), the model's assumptions, and the analysts' assumptions, by using team discussions or requesting information about the rationale for each estimation choice.
- Use historical data and metrics from related or similar programs.

2. System Development

Uncertainties in such areas as planning, scheduling, coordination, analysis of alternatives, risk management, relevant experience, and team performance affect the accuracy of the qualifying factors. Some of these uncertainties can be traced to problems with the system definition, and some can be linked to poor practices in project management or system/software engineering. *Poor practices* refer to development tasks that are not effectively implemented, such as risk management, system integration, and application of software development standards. These uncertainties can translate into erroneous inputs for the estimation data.

Here, too, cost analysts may have little or no influence in rectifying these uncertainties, since the uncertainties are the responsibility of the developer. But an analyst must judge the significance of these uncertainties and account for them in selecting estimation data or in reporting the estimate (for example, by specifying confidence intervals around the estimate).

What are the uncertainties and indicators of risk?

1. Critical-path activities (that is, activities that are essential to project completion, no matter what development process is

chosen) are unknown or unresolvable. Symptoms of this problem include the following:

- There is considerable uncertainty about how much time each activity will take.
- A properly detailed, integrated master schedule or its equivalent does not exist.
- Some tasks have inconsistent or undefined entry and exit criteria.
- All necessary activities are not documented or illustrated.
- Dependencies between tasks are not identified.
- The total critical-path time is equal to or close to the sum of all the most probable times of the steps on the critical path; that is, there is no "slack time."

2. There is a lack of evidence that developers are heeding or will adhere to software management plans. Warning signs include

- Lack of communication between project managers and developers.
- Lack of developer awareness of schedules, deadlines, or milestones.
- Inconsistent understanding and application of the intent of and conformance with software management plans across the development organization.
- Inadequate monitoring, mitigation, and reporting of the project's achievement of planned milestones.

3. No consideration is made about whether it is cheaper to rebuild a component from scratch or to maintain it. A sign of this problem is the following:

- No trade-off analysis exists to demonstrate the decision rationale.

4. Potential defects are not considered. Warning signs of this tunnel vision include

- Not enough time (or no time at all) is allotted in the schedule to repair defects.

- No one knows where defects might occur.

5. The company's record and personnel do not suggest that the software can be completed within the proposed cost and schedule. An indicator of this potential problem is

   - Key personnel or the contractor's previous work is inconsistent with current project needs.

6. Program risks have not been thoroughly assessed. In particular, information about risks, their probabilities of occurrence, and the consequences of loss are not available. Warning signs include

   - Lack of uncertainty bounds (confidence levels and inter vals) in the estimation outputs.
   - Too many point estimates, or the ranges are too narrow.
   - Lack of interest or awareness in risk assessment.

What steps can be taken to address these risks?

- Use ranges for adjustment factors, rather than single values.
- Conduct several estimates over time, to determine whether the organization is improving over time.
- Request additional detail on developing-organization performance, to help quantify a particular risk or set of risks.
- Use historical data and metrics from related or similar developer experiences (from sources other than the developer, if available).
- Review program documentation, such as software-development plans and risk-management plans.

3. Estimation Process

Uncertainties are involved in the selection, application, and interpretation of estimation methods, tools, and data. These decision points directly affect the estimation result, independent of other sources of error. However, poor understanding of the system or the development approach can contribute to the uncertainty, amplifying problems by leading to selecting the wrong estimation method, applying the method incorrectly, or interpreting the results inappropriately. For example, it can be very risky to use linear extrapolation from one set of completed projects to the proposed project when the systems are dramatically different in size, complexity, or some other critical factor.

In this domain, cost analysts may have some control over the outcome. It is the cost analyst's sole responsibility to mitigate these uncertainties via training, use of multiple methods, sensitivity analysis, consulting, and even directing other analysts to redo their estimation.

To more easily understand the uncertainties and indicators of risk in the estimation method, we divide the estimation process into discrete steps according to where the uncertainty or risk may occur:

1. Select methods and tools.
2. Collect data to support the methods and models.
3. Analyze and evaluate the model's results.
4. Analyze documentation of the estimate.

Here, mitigation strategies to address the risks are suggested at the end of the risk list.

Select Methods and Tools

1. There is not enough information about the problem to make a decision about which model or method to use. Warning signs for this risk include

   - The justification for model selection does not include system characteristics (development approach, phase, complexity/size, etc.) as a factor in the selection.
   - Justification for model selection does not include a relative comparison across the set of plausible models.

2. An inappropriate model or method is used to estimate size and cost. Symptoms of this problem include

- The model or method generates intermediate results that seem inconsistent with developers' experience or expectations.
- The model cannot be configured to reflect the development approach (such as waterfall, spiral/iterative, incremental) or calibrated to the system characteristics (because there are no underlying data sets).

3. An appropriate model is used, but it is used incorrectly to generate erroneous results. This risk is high if

 - The model or method generates intermediate results that seem inconsistent with developers' experience or expectations.
 - The model cannot be configured to reflect the development approach (such as waterfall, spiral/iterative, incremental) or calibrated to the system characteristics (because there are no underlying data sets).

4. The model chosen was created with one type of development in mind, which is not applicable to the project for which the contractors are bidding. Signs that such a problem is occurring include

 - The current project at hand falls outside the boundary of the model's capability in terms of size, development type, or life-cycle phase.
 - Model users find themselves being asked to enter irrelevant inputs.

5. The model chosen does not adequately consider maintenance costs and time. Warning signs include

 - The model generates intermediate results that seem too low in comparison with developers' experience or expectations.
 - The justification for model selection did not compare the model's capability to the system-development phases for which it is needed.

6. The capabilities of the model are not consistent with the intended use of the estimate.[7] Symptoms of this problem include the following:

   - The expected use for the estimate is not known or was not considered in the model-selection decision process.
   - The available models have not been evaluated to determine what estimating objectives they support.

Collect Data for Model

7. There is not enough information about variables to enter a value in the model. This problem has arisen if the following situations are occurring:

   - There is significant use of default values for inputs.
   - The justification for parameter values is not based on or consistent with what is observed or anticipated in system development.

8. Input values for the cost and schedule data are incomplete or erroneous. Symptoms include

   - The model generates results that seem inconsistent with developers' experience or expectations.
   - There are many blank spaces in the database of supporting information.

9. Inconsistent data inputs (combinations and model parameters that indicate inconsistency) are used in the model: Indications are

   - Obviously flawed outputs, or outputs that seem inconsistent with user's expectations.
   - Different people are using the model at the same time for the same calculation.

---

[7] An Institute for Defense Analyses (IDA) report (Bailey et al., 1986) identified five general uses for estimation models. For each use, the report described criteria to help an analyst determine the model's relative applicability for a given usage.

- People who are working on different parts of the project (to generate the input numbers) have not communicated with each other to make sure their results are consistent.

Analyze and Evaluate Model's Results

10. The model presents an unreasonable picture of likely cost and schedule. This situation may arise if the following symptoms are apparent:

   - None of the proposals contains estimates close to the buyer's expected cost or schedule.
   - Expected cost and schedule do not seem realistic in the minds of managers or staff, judging from their prior experience with project budgets and time frames.

11. The model is used incorrectly to show areas of greatest uncertainty or to suggest the consequences of risk. This situation may be occurring if

   - The model generates results that seem inconsistent with developers' experience or expectations of what areas have considerable uncertainty.

12. The model is used incorrectly to determine key cost factors, as indicated by the following warning sign:

   - The model generates results that seem inconsistent with developers' experience or expectations of what key cost factors are likely to be.

Analyze the Documentation

13. There is no record of past and current cost and schedule projections, nor are there comparisons with actual completion cost and time. This situation may occur if

   - There is a lack of time to compare current project information with past projects or to reveal past flaws in estimation.

- There are significant obstacles to comparing current information with past projections and actual costs or schedules.

14. The data for purposes of comparison are not available or not sought, as indicated by the following warning signs:

- There is a lack of time to compare current project information with past projects or to reveal past flaws in estimation.
- There are significant obstacles to comparing current information with past projections and actual costs or schedules.

What steps can be taken to address these risks?

- Before it is needed, garner as much information as possible about the project.
- Take time to understand what methods each model uses, and whether those methods/models are appropriate to the project at hand.
- Ensure that staff is trained on how to use each model.
- Generate reasonable estimates for each model variable, preferably in advance of examining the contractor data. If possible, conduct a sensitivity analysis on those key variables that engender significant uncertainty.
- Understand and document all the assumptions of the selected estimation model.
- Use correct and appropriate economic data, such as cost rates for personnel, to support each model input. Pay careful attention to the scale or units required for each variable, such as constant dollars or dollars adjusted for inflation.
- Understand whether and how each method or model considers maintenance costs and time, and adjust accordingly.
- Develop and retain a repository of historical data and metrics. Then use the data to support realistic inputs, to check the realism of outputs, and to provide feedback, learning, and comparison.

- Simplify models where possible, by concentrating on using inputs with the most effect and eliminating inputs that have very little effect on the resulting estimate. The effect of each input can be assessed retrospectively by performing a sensitivity analysis on each input; those whose differences yield little change in the overall estimate can be eliminated in future estimates.
- Use multiple models to "triangulate" a reasonable estimate. In addition, verify reasonableness with expert judgment.

CHAPTER EIGHT

Final Directions

Cost analysts have a difficult task: to make important quantitative decisions about large systems, often based on little information and with a great deal of uncertainty. This document is focused on helping them identify the uncertainty inherent in producing or evaluating a software size or cost estimate and to find ways to reduce or at least manage that uncertainty. To do so, we have reviewed a number of typical size- and cost-estimation methods, noting in each instance the basis for the technique and the appropriate ways to use it. At the same time, we have discussed various issues that arise in deciding which method to use, and we have developed checklists to help analysts recognize and mitigate the risks involved. The point is not to pick the "right" estimation method but to reduce the risk and uncertainty wherever possible by understanding the issues involved in performing the estimation.

The information in this document can be used in two ways: to address techniques for improving current estimation methods and to find new methods when existing ones prove inadequate. The latter function is particularly important. Software development is changing, reflecting not only the need to find better ways to build better software but also the market pressures to use different technologies as they are proposed by the research and commercial communities. For these reasons, it is essential that estimation-analysis organizations maintain historical records of their success with a variety of methods in a variety of contexts. In addition to the expected variation due to the ways in which different people use different estimation methods, there is variation due to the appropriateness of a technique and to the correctness with which it is applied. A repository of information about what technique was used, in what way, and with what degree of success can assist analysts in making decisions about the best ways to reduce uncertainty in estimates and the necessity of developing new estimation techniques from time to time.

Cost analysts can use their past history to predict the future—to provide confidence intervals around estimates, and to take action when values fall outside of the confidence limits. An inaccurate estimate does not always mean a bad estimating technique or an incapable analyst. Instead, it may mean that the technique must be calibrated or extended, or that the analyst may need refresher training. Moreover, the literature on decisionmaking suggests that the broader the experience base of the analyst, the more likely it is that the analyst will understand the variability among systems.

The U.S. Air Force and others can combine the checklists in this document with a quantitative history and careful resource planning to provide analysts with the variety of estimating experiences they need to become better cost analysts.

References

Albrecht, Allan J., "Measuring Application Development," *Proceedings of the IBM Applications Development Joint SHARE/GUIDE Symposium*, Monterey, Calif., 1979, pp. 83–92.

Albrecht, Allan J., and John E. Gaffney, "Software Function, Source Lines of Code, and Development Effort Prediction," *IEEE Transactions on Software Engineering*, Vol. SE-9, No. 6, November 1983, pp. 639–647.

Bailey, E. K., T. P. Frazier, and J. W. Bailey, "A Descriptive Evaluation of Automated Software Cost-Estimation Models." Washington, D.C.: Office of the Assistant Secretary of Defense (Comptroller) and Institute for Defense Analyses (IDA), IDA Paper P-1979, 1986.

Banker, R. D., R. J. Kauffman, and R. Kumar, "An Empirical Test of Object-Based Output Measurement Metrics in a Computer Aided Software Engineering Environment," *Journal of Management Information Systems*, Vol. 8, No. 3, Winter 1991–1992, pp. 127–150.

Banker, R. D., and C. F. Kemerer, "Scale Economies in New Software Development," *IEEE Transactions on Software Engineering*, Vol. 15, No. 10, 1989, pp. 199–204.

Boehm, Barry W., Chris Abts, A. Winsor Brown, Sunita Chulani, Bradford K. Clark, Ellis Horowitz, Ray Madachy, Donald Reifer, and Bert Steece, *Software Cost Estimation with COCOMO II,* Upper Saddle River, N.J.: Prentice Hall, 2000.

Booch, Grady, *Object-oriented Analysis with Applications*, 2nd ed., Redwood City, Calif.: Benjamin Cummings, 1994.

Briand, Lionel, Khaled El Emam, Dagmar Surmann, Isabella Wieczorek, and Katrina Maxwell, *An Assessment and Comparison of Common Software*

Cost Modeling Techniques, Kaiserslautern, Germany: Fraunhofer Center for Empirical Software Engineering, ISERN technical report 98-27, 1998.

Carleton, Anita D., Robert E. Park, and Wolfhart B. Goethert, "The SEO Core Measures: Background Information and Recommendations for Use and Implementation," *Crosstalk*, May 1994. Available at http://www.stsc.hill.af.mil/crosstalk/1994/05/xt94d05c.asp.

Carleton, Anita D., Robert E. Park, Wolfhart Goethert, William Florac, Elizabeth Bailey, and Shari Lawrence Pfleeger, "Software Measurement for DoD Systems: Recommendations for Initial Core Measures," Pittsburgh, Pa.: Carnegie Mellon University, Software Engineering Institute, CMU/SEI-92-TR-19, September 1992.

Chidamber, Shyam R., and Chris F. Kemerer, "A Metrics Suite for Object-oriented Design", *IEEE Transactions on Software Engineering*, Vol. 20, No. 6, June 1994, pp. 476–493.

Cook, Cynthia, and John C. Graser, *Military Airframe Acquisition Costs: The Effects of Lean Manufacturing*, Santa Monica, Calif.: RAND Corporation, MR-1325-AF, 2001.

Fenton, Norman, and Shari Lawrence Pfleeger, *Software Metrics: A Rigorous and Practical Approach*, 2nd ed., Florence, Ky.: Brooks Cole, 1996.

Fox, Bernard, Michael Boito, John C. Graser, and Obaid Younossi, *Test and Evaluation Trends and Costs for Aircraft and Guided Weapons*, Santa Monica, Calif.: RAND Corporation, MG-109-AF, 2004.

Divinagracia, Harvey Roy, *Function Point Calculator*, Dearborn, Mich: University of Michigan. Available at http://www.engin.umd.umich.edu/CIS/course.des/cis525/js/f00/harvey/FP_Calc.html.

Galorath Incorporated, *Software Size Analysis for Integrated Logistics System-Supply (ILS-S)*, El Segundo, Calif., Revised Report for Air Force Cost Analysis Agency, June 21, 2002.

Hancock, W. C., "Practical Applications of Three Basic Algorithms in Estimating Software Cost," in R. Goldberg and H. Lorin, eds., *The Economics of Information Processing*, New York: Wiley Interscience, 1982.

IEEE Computer Society, *IEEE Standard 729: Glossary of Software Engineering Terminology*, Los Alamitos, Calif: IEEE Computer Society Press, 1983.

International Function Point User's Group, http://www.ifpug.org.

International Function Point Users Group, *Function Point Counting Practices Manual,* Release 4.1.1, Princeton Junction, N.J., 2001.

International Function Point Users Group, *Guidelines to Software Measurement,* Release 1.1, Princeton Junction, N.J., 2001.

Jeffery, D. Ross, Graham C. Low, and Michael Barnes, "A Comparison of Function Point Counting Techniques," *IEEE Transactions on Software Engineering,* Vol. 19, No. 5, 1993, pp. 529–532.

Kauffman R. J., and R. Kumar, "Modeling Estimation Expertise in Object-based CASE Environments," New York: New York University, Stern School of Business Report, January 1993.

Kitchenham, Barbara A., and Kari Känsälä, "Inter-item Correlations Among Function Points," *Proceedings of the 15th International Conference on Software Engineering,* Los Alamitos, Calif.: IEEE Computer Society Press, 1993, pp. 477–480.

Kitchenham, Barbara A., Shari Lawrence Pfleeger, and Norman Fenton, "Towards a Framework for Software Measurement Validation," *IEEE Transactions on Software Engineering,* Vol. 21, No. 12, December 1995, pp. 929–943.

Lorell, Mark, and John C. Graser, *An Overview of Acquisition Reform Cost Savings Estimates,* Santa Monica, Calif.: RAND Corporation, MR-1329-AF, 2001.

Low, Graham C., and D. Ross Jeffery, "Calibrating Estimation Tools for Software Development," *Software Engineering Journal,* Vol. 5, No. 4, 1990, pp. 215–221.

MacDonell, Stephen, Martin Shepperd, and Peter Sallis, "Metrics for Database Systems: An Empirical Study," *Proceedings of the Fourth IEEE International Symposium on Software Metrics,* Albuquerque, N.M., 1997.

Merriam-Webster, *Merriam-Webster's Collegiate Dictionary,* 11th ed., Springfield, Mass., 2003.

Minkiewicz, Arlene F., *Measuring Object-Oriented Software with Predictive Object Points,* report for Price-S Systems, n.d. Available at http://www.pricesystems.com/downloads/pdf/pops.pdf.

Morgan, M. Granger, and Max Henrion, *Uncertainty,* Cambridge, England: Cambridge University Press, 1990.

National Aeronautics and Space Administration (NASA), *NASA Cost Estimation Handbook*, 2002. Available at http://www.jsc.nasa.gov/bu2/NCEH/NASA%20CEH%20Final%20Production%20Copy%20April%202002.pdf.

Norden, Peter, and A. V. Bakshi, "Internal Dynamics of Research and Development Projects," *Management Sciences Models and Techniques*, New York: Pergamon Press, 1960, pp. 187–205.

Park, Robert E., *A Manager's Checklist for Validating Software Cost and Schedule Estimates*, Pittsburgh, Pa.: Carnegie Mellon University, Software Engineering Institute, special report CMU/SEI-95-SR-004, January 1995.

Park, Robert E., *Software Size Measurement: A Framework for Counting Source Statements*, Pittsburgh, Pa.: Carnegie Mellon University, Software Engineering Institute, CMU/SEI-92-TR-20, September 1992.

Pfleeger, Shari Lawrence, and Joanne M. Atlee, *Software Engineering: Theory and Practice*, 3rd ed., Upper Saddle River, N.J.: Prentice Hall, 2005.

Putnam, Lawrence, "A General Empirical Solution to the Macro Software Sizing and Estimating Problem," *IEEE Transactions on Software Engineering*, Vol. 2, No. 2, 1978, pp. 345–361.

Sackman, H. H., W. J. Erikson, and E. E. Grant, "Exploratory Experimental Studies Comparing Online and Offline Programming Performance," *Communications of the ACM*, Vol. 11, No. 1, January 1968, pp. 3–11.

Shepperd, Martin, and Chris Schofield, "Estimating Software Project Effort Using Analogies," *IEEE Transactions on Software Engineering*, Vol. 23, No. 12, November 1997, pp. 736–743.

Software Productivity Research, "What Are Feature Points?" n.d. Available at http://www.spr.com/products/feature.shtm.

Stensrud, Eric, "Estimating with Enhanced Object Points vs. Function Points," *Proceedings of the 13th COCOMO/SCM Forum*, Los Angeles, Calif.: University of Southern California, October 1998.

Younossi, Obaid, Mark V. Arena, Richard M. Moore, Mark Lorell, Joanna Mason, and John C. Graser, *Military Jet Engine Acquisition: Technology Basics and Cost-Estimating Methodology*, Santa Monica, Calif.: RAND Corporation, MR-1596-AF, 2002.

Younossi, Obaid, Michael Kennedy, and John C. Graser, *Military Airframe Costs: The Effects of Advanced Materials and Manufacturing Processes*, Santa Monica, Calif.: RAND Corporation, MR-1370-AF, 2001.